ROMEO AND JULIET

ROMEO AND JULIET

William Shakespeare

WORDSWORTH CLASSICS

This edition published 1992
by Wordsworth Editions Limited
Cumberland House, Crib Street, Ware,
Hertfordshire SG12 9ET

ISBN 1-85326-014-2

*Printed and bound in Great Britain
by Mackays of Chatham plc, Chatham, Kent*

INTRODUCTION

The plot of *Romeo and Juliet* is a familiar one. It is anticipated by many stories of doomed love; Samson and Delilah, Paris and Helen and Abelard and Heloise spring to mind. It is the age-old story of love reaching across the barriers of family and convention, in which young Romeo Montague falls in love with Lord Capulet's daughter Juliet. These two foremost families of Verona are bitter rivals, and the scandalous liaison causes a deadly quarrel in which members of both houses are killed. The lovers contrive to marry and spend a blissful night in each other's arms, but after an enforced parting a series of misunderstandings result in the suicides of both Romeo and Juliet. Their tragic deaths reconcile the Montagues and the Capulets, and peace is restored to Verona.

In the bad quarto of 1597, the play is entitled 'An excellent conceited Tragedie of Romeo and Juliet' and it is Shakespeare's first romantic tragedy (cf *Troilus and Cressida* 1602). It is easy to see the play as a banal expression of the romantic love that was fashionable towards the end of the 16th century, and which is characterised by the sonnet craze of the 1590's. The play derives from the Italian short story conventions of Bandello and Salernitano, and is based on Arthur Brooke's *Tragical History of Romeus and Juliet* (1562) but it succeeds in rising above the traditional tale of adolescent love by its moving language which, for all its grandeur of expression, is basically simple. Because of the timelessness of the plot, it is one of the most approachable of Shakespeare's plays, and the attractions of the story have found expression in opera and ballet as well as in some of the more glutinous offerings of Hollywood.

Details of William Shakespeare's early life are scanty. He was the son of a prosperous merchant of Stratford upon Avon, and tradition has it that he was born on 23rd April 1564; records show that he was baptized three days later. It is likely that he attended the local Grammar School, but he had no university education. Of his early career there is no record, though John Aubrey states that he was a country schoolmaster. How he became involved with the stage is equally uncertain, but he was sufficiently established as a play-wright by 1592 to be criticized in print. He was a leading member of the Lord Chamberlain's Company, which became the King's

Men on the accession of James I in 1603. Shakespeare married Anne Hathaway in 1582, by whom he had two daughters and a son, Hamnet, who died in 1586. Towards the end of his life he loosened his ties with London, and retired to New Place, his substantial property in Stratford which he had bought in 1597. He died on 23rd April 1616 aged 52, and is buried in Holy Trinity Church, Stratford.

Further reading:

N Brooke: Shakespeare's Early Tragedies 1968
R Nevo: Tragic Form in Shakespeare 1972
F E Halliday: A Shakespeare Companion rev 1964
The Cambridge Companion to Shakespeare Studies 1986

The scene: Verona and Mantua

CHARACTERS IN THE PLAY

ESCALUS, *prince of Verona*
PARIS, *a young nobleman, kinsman to the prince*
MONTAGUE } *heads of two houses at enmity with each*
CAPULET }   *other*
An old man, kinsman to Capulet
ROMEO, *son to Montague*
MERCUTIO, *kinsman to the prince, and friend to Romeo*
BENVOLIO, *nephew to Montague, and friend to Romeo*
TYBALT, *nephew to Lady Capulet*
FRIAR LAWRENCE, *a Franciscan*
FRIAR JOHN, *of the same order*
BALTHASAR, *servant to Romeo*
SAMPSON }
GREGORY } *servants to Capulet*
PETER, *servant to Juliet's Nurse*
ABRAHAM, *servant to Montague*
An Apothecary
Three Musicians
Page to Paris, another Page, an Officer
LADY MONTAGUE, *wife to Montague*
LADY CAPULET, *wife to Capulet*
JULIET, *daughter to Capulet*
Nurse to Juliet

Citizens, Kinsfolk of both houses, Guards, Watchmen, Servants and Attendants

CHORUS

ROMEO AND JULIET

ROMEO AND JULIET

The Prologue

Enter Chorus

Chorus. Two households, both alike in dignity,
  In fair Verona, where we lay our scene,
From ancient grudge break to new mutiny,
  Where civil blood makes civil hands unclean.
From forth the fatal loins of these two foes
  A pair of star-crossed lovers take their life;
Whose misadventured piteous overthrows
  Doth with their death bury their parents' strife.
The fearful passage of their death-marked love,
  And the continuance of their parents' rage,   10
Which, but their children's end, nought could remove,
  Is now the two hours' traffic of our stage;
The which if you with patient ears attend,
What here shall miss, our toil shall strive to mend.

                        [exit

[1. 1.]   *Verona. A public place*

  'Enter SAMPSON and GREGORY of the house of
      CAPULET, with swords and bucklers'

Sampson. Gregory, on my word we'll not carry coals.
Gregory. No, for then we should be colliers.
Sampson. I mean, an we be in choler we'll draw.
Gregory. Ay, while you live draw your neck out of collar.

Sampson. I strike quickly, being moved.

Gregory. But thou art not quickly moved to strike.

Sampson. A dog of the house of Montague moves me.

Gregory. To move is to stir, and to be valiant is to
10 stand: therefore if thou art moved thou runn'st away.

Sampson. A dog of that house shall move me to stand:
I will take the wall of any man or maid of Montague's.

Gregory. That shows thee a weak slave, for the
weakest goes to the wall.

Sampson. 'Tis true, and therefore women, being the
weaker vessels, are ever thrust to the wall: therefore
I will push Montague's men from the wall, and thrust
his maids to the wall.

Gregory. The quarrel is between our masters, and us
20 their men.

Sampson. 'Tis all one; I will show myself a tyrant:
when I have fought with the men, I will be cruel with
the maids; I will cut off their heads.

Gregory. The heads of the maids?

Sampson. Ay, the heads of the maids, or their maiden-
heads; take it in what sense thou wilt.

Gregory. They must take it in sense that feel it.

Sampson. Me they shall feel while I am able to stand,
and 'tis known I am a pretty piece of flesh.

30 *Gregory.* 'Tis well thou art not fish; if thou hadst,
thou hadst been poor John. Draw thy tool; here comes
two of the house of Montagues.

Enter ABRAHAM and another serving man

Sampson. My naked weapon is out: quarrel; I will
back thee.

Gregory. How? Turn thy back and run?

Sampson. Fear me not.

Gregory. No, marry; I fear thee!

Sampson. Let us take the law of our sides; let them begin.

Gregory. I will frown as I pass by, and let them take it 40 as they list.

Sampson. Nay, as they dare. I will bite my thumb at them, which is disgrace to them if they bear it.

Abraham. Do you bite your thumb at us, sir?

Sampson. I do bite my thumb, sir.

Abraham. Do you bite your thumb at us, sir?

(*Sampson.* Is the law of our side if I say ay?

(*Gregory.* No.

Sampson. No, sir, I do not bite my thumb at you, sir, but I bite my thumb, sir. 50

Gregory. Do you quarrel, sir?

Abraham. Quarrel, sir? No, sir.

Sampson. But if you do, sir, I am for you: I serve as good a man as you.

Abraham. No better.

Sampson. Well, sir.

'*Enter* BENVOLIO' *on one side,* TYBALT *on the other*

(*Gregory* [*seeing Tybalt*]. Say 'better': here comes one of my master's kinsmen.

Sampson. Yes, better, sir.

Abraham. You lie. 60

Sampson. Draw, if you be men. Gregory, remember thy washing blow. ['*they fight*'

Benvolio [*intervening from behind*]. Part, fools!
Put up your swords; you know not what you do.

TYBALT *comes up*

Tybalt. What, art thou drawn among these
  heartless hinds?
Turn thee, Benvolio; look upon thy death.

Benvolio. I do but keep the peace: put up
    thy sword,
Or manage it to part these men with me.
    Tybalt. What, drawn, and talk of peace? I hate
    the word,
70 As I hate hell, all Montagues, and thee:
Have at thee, coward.

*They fight. Enter several of both houses, joining in the
fray. Then 'enter three or four Citizens with clubs or
partisans', and an Officer*

    Officer. Clubs, bills, and partisans! Strike, beat
    them down.
Down with the Capulets, down with the Montagues!

'Enter old CAPULET *in his gown, and his wife'*

Capulet. What noise is this? Give me my long
    sword, ho!
Lady Capulet. A crutch, a crutch! Why call you for
    a sword?
Capulet. My sword, I say! Old Montague is come,
And flourishes his blade in spite of me.

'Enter old MONTAGUE *and his wife'*

Montague. Thou villain Capulet!—Hold me not, let
    me go.
Lady Montague. Thou shalt not stir one foot to seek
    a foe.

'Enter PRINCE ESCALUS, *with his train'*

80 *Prince.* Rebellious subjects, enemies to peace,
Profaners of this neighbour-stainéd steel,—
Will they not hear? What ho! you men, you beasts,
That quench the fire of your pernicious rage

With purple fountains issuing from your veins,
On pain of torture, from those bloody hands
Throw your mistempered weapons to the ground,
And hear the sentence of your movéd prince.
Three civil brawls, bred of an airy word
By thee, old Capulet, and Montague,
Have thrice disturbed the quiet of our streets,   90
And made Verona's ancient citizens
Cast by their grave beseeming ornaments
To wield old partisans, in hands as old,
Cankered with peace, to part your cankered hate:
If ever you disturb our streets again,
Your lives shall pay the forfeit of the peace.
For this time, all the rest depart away:
You, Capulet, shall go along with me;
And, Montague, come you this afternoon,
To know our farther pleasure in this case,   100
To old Freetown, our common judgement-place.
Once more, on pain of death, all men depart.
[*all but Montague, Lady Montague, and Benvolio depart*
  Montague. Who set this ancient quarrel new abroach?
Speak, nephew, were you by when it began?
  Benvolio. Here were the servants of your adversary
And yours, close fighting ere I did approach:
I drew to part them; in the instant came
The fiery Tybalt, with his sword prepared,
Which, as he breathed defiance to my ears,
He swung about his head, and cut the winds,   110
Who, nothing hurt withal, hissed him in scorn:
While we were interchanging thrusts and blows,
Came more and more, and fought on part and part,
Till the prince came, who parted either part.
  Lady Montague. O where is Romeo? Saw you
      him today?

Right glad I am he was not at this fray.
  Benvolio. Madam, an hour before the
    worshipped sun
Peered forth the golden window of the east,
A troubled mind drave me to walk abroad,
120 Where, underneath the grove of sycamore
That westward rooteth from this city's side,
So early walking did I see your son:
Towards him I made, but he was ware of me,
And stole into the covert of the wood:
I, measuring his affections by my own,
Which then most sought where most might not
    be found,
Being one too many by my weary self,
Pursued my humour, not pursuing his,
And gladly shunned who gladly fled from me.
130   *Montague.* Many a morning hath he there
    been seen,
With tears augmenting the fresh morning's dew,
Adding to clouds more clouds with his deep sighs;
But all so soon as the all-cheering sun
Should in the farthest east begin to draw
The shady curtains from Aurora's bed,
Away from light steals home my heavy son,
And private in his chamber pens himself,
Shuts up his windows, locks fair daylight out,
And makes himself an artificial night:
140 Black and portentous must this humour prove,
Unless good counsel may the cause remove.
  Benvolio. My noble uncle, do you know the cause?
  Montague. I neither know it, nor can learn
    of him.
  Benvolio. Have you importuned him by
    any means?

Montague. Both by myself and many other friends:
But he, his own affections' counsellor,
Is to himself—I will not say how true—
But to himself so secret and so close,
So far from sounding and discovery,
As is the bud bit with an envious worm,   150
Ere he can spread his sweet leaves to the air,
Or dedicate his beauty to the sun.
Could we but learn from whence his sorrows grow,
We would as willingly give cure as know.

'*Enter* ROMEO'

Benvolio. See where he comes: so please you,
  step aside;
I'll know his grievance or be much denied.
Montague. I would thou wert so happy by thy stay
To hear true shrift. Come, madam, let's away.
                    [*Montague and his wife depart*
Benvolio. Good morrow, cousin.
Romeo.   Is the day so young?
Benvolio. But new struck nine.
Romeo.   Ay me, sad hours seem long. 160
Was that my father that went hence so fast?
Benvolio. It was. What sadness lengthens
  Romeo's hours?
Romeo. Not having that which, having, makes
  them short.
Benvolio. In love?
Romeo. Out—
Benvolio. Of love?
Romeo. Out of her favour where I am in love.
Benvolio. Alas that Love, so gentle in his view,
Should be so tyrannous and rough in proof!
Romeo. Alas that Love, whose view is muffled still.   170

Should without eyes see pathways to his will!
Where shall we dine?—O me! What fray
    was here?
Yet tell me not, for I have heard it all:
Here's much to do with hate, but more with love:
Why, then, O brawling love, O loving hate,
O anything of nothing first create!
O heavy lightness, serious vanity,
Misshapen chaos of well-seeming forms,
Feather of lead, bright smoke, cold fire,
    sick health,
180 Still-waking sleep, that is not what it is!
This love feel I, that feel no love in this.
Dost thou not laugh?
    Benvolio.   No, coz, I rather weep.
    Romeo. Good heart, at what?
    Benvolio.   At thy good heart's oppression.
    Romeo. Why, such is love's transgression.
Griefs of mine own lie heavy in my breast,
Which thou wilt propagate, to have it pressed
With more of thine. This love that thou hast shown
Doth add more grief to too much of mine own.
Love is a smoke made with the fume of sighs:
190 Being purged, a fire sparkling in lovers' eyes;
Being vexed, a sea nourished with lovers' tears.
What is it else? A madness most discreet,
A choking gall and a preserving sweet.
Farewell, my coz.
    Benvolio.   Soft, I will go along:
And if you leave me so, you do me wrong.
    Romeo. Tut, I have lost myself, I am not here,
This is not Romeo, he's some other where.
    Benvolio. Tell me in sadness, who is that you love?
    Romeo. What, shall I groan and tell thee?

Benvolio.   Groan? Why no:
But sadly tell me, who?   200
  Romeo. Bid a sick man in sadness make his will—
A word ill urged to one that is so ill.
In sadness, cousin, I do love a woman.
  Benvolio. I aimed so near when I supposed
          you loved.
  Romeo. A right good markman! And she's fair
          I love.
  Benvolio. A right fair mark, fair coz, is soonest hit.
  Romeo. Well, in that hit you miss. She'll not be hit
With Cupid's arrow: she hath Dian's wit,
And, in strong proof of chastity well armed,
From Love's weak childish bow she lives unharmed.   210
She will not stay the siege of loving terms,
Nor bide th'encounter of assailing eyes,
Nor ope her lap to saint-seducing gold.
O, she is rich in beauty, only poor
That, when she dies, with beauty dies her store.
  Benvolio. Then she hath sworn that she will still
          live chaste?
  Romeo. She hath, and in that sparing makes
          huge waste:
For beauty, starved with her severity,
Cuts beauty off from all posterity.
She is too fair, too wise, wisely too fair.   220
To merit bliss by making me despair:
She hath forsworn to love, and in that vow
Do I live dead, that live to tell it now.
  Benvolio. Be ruled by me; forget to think of her.
  Romeo. O, teach me how I should forget to think.
  Benvolio. By giving liberty unto thine eyes;
Examine other beauties.
  Romeo.   'Tis the way

To call hers (exquisite) in question more.
These happy masks that kiss fair ladies' brows,
230 Being black, puts us in mind they hide the fair.
He that is strucken blind cannot forget
The precious treasure of his eyesight lost.
Show me a mistress that is passing fair:
What doth her beauty serve but as a note
Where I may read who passed that passing fair?
Farewell, thou canst not teach me to forget.

Benvolio. I'll pay that doctrine, or else die in debt.

[*they go*

[1. 2.]   *The same; later in the day*

'*Enter* CAPULET, *County* PARIS, *and the* CLOWN',
servant to Capulet

Capulet. But Montague is bound as well as I,
In penalty alike; and 'tis not hard, I think,
For men so old as we to keep the peace.
Paris. Of honourable reckoning are you both,
And pity 'tis you lived at odds so long.
But now, my lord, what say you to my suit?
Capulet. But saying o'er what I have said before:
My child is yet a stranger in the world;
She hath not seen the change of fourteen years:
10 Let two more summers wither in their pride
Ere we may think her ripe to be a bride.
Paris. Younger than she are happy mothers made.
Capulet. And too soon marred are those so
    early made.
Earth hath swallowed all my hopes but she;
She is the hopeful lady of my earth.
But woo her, gentle Paris, get her heart;

My will to her consent is but a part:
And, she agreed, within her scope of choice
Lies my consent and fair according voice.
This night I hold an old accustomed feast,   20
Whereto I have invited many a guest,
Such as I love; and you among the store,
One more most welcome, makes my number more.
At my poor house look to behold this night
Earth-treading stars that make dark heaven light.
Such comfort as do lusty young men feel
When well-apparelled April on the heel
Of limping winter treads, even such delight
Among fresh female buds shall you this night
Inherit at my house: hear all, all see,   30
And like her most whose merit most shall be:
Which on more view, of many mine being one
May stand in number, though in reckoning none.
Come, go with me. [*To the Clown*] Go, sirrah,
        trudge about
Through fair Verona; find those persons out
Whose names are written there, [*giving him a paper*]
        and to them say
My house and welcome on their pleasure stay.
                        [*Capulet and Paris go*
Clown [*turns the paper about*]. Find them out whose
names are written here! It is written that the shoemaker
should meddle with his yard and the tailor with his last,   40
the fisher with his pencil and the painter with his nets.
But I am sent to find those persons whose names are
here writ, and can never find what names the writing
person hath here writ. I must to the learned. In good
time!

'*Enter* BENVOLIO *and* ROMEO'

Benvolio. Tut, man, one fire burns out
    another's burning,
One pain is lessened by another's anguish;
Turn giddy, and be holp by backward turning;
One desperate grief cures with another's languish;
50 Take thou some new infection to thy eye,
And the rank poison of the old will die.
    Romeo. Your plantain leaf is excellent for that.
    Benvolio. For what, I pray thee?
    Romeo.   For your broken shin.
    Benvolio. Why, Romeo, art thou mad?
    Romeo. Not mad, but bound more than a madman is:
Shut up in prison, kept without my food,
Whipped and tormented, and—God-den,
    good fellow.
    Clown. God gi' god-den. I pray, sir, can you read?
    Romeo. Ay, mine own fortune in my misery.
60   *Clown.* Perhaps you have learned it without book:
but, I pray, can you read anything you see?
    Romeo. Ay, if I know the letters and the language.
    Clown. Ye say honestly: rest you merry.
                                 [*he turns to go*
    Romeo. Stay, fellow; I can read.   [*he reads the list*
'Signior Martino and his wife and daughters,
County Anselmo and his beauteous sisters,
The lady widow of Vitruvio,
Signior Placentio and his lovely nieces,
Mercutio and his brother Valentine,
70 Mine uncle Capulet, his wife and daughters,
My fair niece Rosaline and Livia,
Signior Valentio and his cousin Tybalt,
Lucio and the lively Helena.'

A fair assembly: whither should they come?

Clown. Up.

Romeo. Whither?

Clown. To supper; to our house.

Romeo. Whose house?

Clown. My master's.

Romeo. Indeed I should have asked thee that before. 80

Clown. Now I'll tell you without asking. My master
is the great rich Capulet; and, if you be not of the house
of Montagues, I pray come and crush a cup of wine.
Rest you merry.   [*goes*

Benvolio. At this same ancient feast of Capulet's
Sups the fair Rosaline whom thou so loves,
With all the admiréd beauties of Verona:
Go thither, and with unattainted eye
Compare her face with some that I shall show,
And I will make thee think thy swan a crow.   90

Romeo. When the devout religion of mine eye
Maintains such falsehood, then turn tears to fires:
And these who, often drowned, could never die,
Transparent heretics, be burnt for liars.
One fairer than my love! The all-seeing sun
Ne'er saw her match since first the world begun.

Benvolio. Tut, you saw her fair, none else being by,
Herself poised with herself in either eye:
But in that crystal scales let there be weighed
Your lady's love against some other maid   100
That I will show you shining at this feast,
And she shall scant show well that now seems best.

Romeo. I'll go along, no such sight to be shown,
But to rejoice in splendour of mine own.   [*they go*

Within Capulet's house

'Enter Capulet's Wife, and NURSE*'*

Lady Capulet. Nurse, where's my daughter? Call her
    forth to me.
Nurse. Now, by my maidenhead at twelve year old,
I bade her come. What, lamb! What, lady-bird!
God forbid! Where's this girl? What, Juliet!

'Enter JULIET*'*

Juliet. How now, who calls?
Nurse. Your mother.
Juliet. Madam, I am here. What is your will?
Lady Capulet. This is the matter. Nurse, give
    leave awhile:
We must talk in secret. Nurse, come back again:
10 I have remembered me; thou's hear our counsel.
Thou knowest my daughter's of a pretty age.
    Nurse. Faith, I can tell her age unto an hour.
    Lady Capulet. She's not fourteen.
    Nurse.   I'll lay fourteen of my teeth—
And yet, to my teen be it spoken, I have but four—
She's not fourteen. How long is it now
To Lammas-tide?
    Lady Capulet.   A fortnight and odd days.
    Nurse. Even or odd, of all days in the year,
Come Lammas-Eve at night shall she be fourteen.
Susan and she—God rest all Christian souls—
20 Were of an age. Well, Susan is with God;
She was too good for me. But, as I said,
On Lammas-Eve at night shall she be fourteen:
That shall she, marry; I remember it well.
'Tis since the earthquake now eleven years,

And she was weaned—I never shall forget it—
Of all the days of the year, upon that day:
For I had then laid wormwood to my dug,
Sitting in the sun under the dove-house wall.
My lord and you were then at Mantua—
Nay, I do bear a brain! But, as I said,   30
When it did taste the wormwood on the nipple
Of my dug, and felt it bitter, pretty fool,
To see it tetchy and fall out with the dug!
'Shake,' quoth the dove-house: 'twas no need, I trow,
To bid me trudge.
And since that time it is eleven years:
For then she could stand high-lone; nay, by th' rood,
She could have run and waddled all about:
For even the day before, she broke her brow,
And then my husband—God be with his soul,   40
'A was a merry man—took up the child:
'Yea,' quoth he, 'dost thou fall upon thy face?
Thou wilt fall backward when thou hast more wit;
Wilt thou not, Jule?' And, by my holidame,
The pretty wretch left crying, and said 'Ay'.
To see now how a jest shall come about!
I warrant, an I should live a thousand years,
I never should forget it: 'Wilt thou not, Jule?'
     quoth he;
And, pretty fool, it stinted, and said 'Ay'.
  Lady Capulet. Enough of this; I pray thee hold
     thy peace.   50
  Nurse. Yes, madam, yet I cannot choose but laugh,
To think it should leave crying, and say 'Ay':
And yet, I warrant, it had upon it brow
A bump as big as a young cockerel's stone,
A perilous knock: and it cried bitterly.
'Yea', quoth my husband, 'fallst upon thy face?

Thou wilt fall backward when thou comest to age:
Wilt thou not, Jule?' It stinted, and said 'Ay'.
Juliet. And stint thou too, I pray thee, Nurse, say I.
60 *Nurse.* Peace, I have done. God mark thee to
    his grace!
Thou wast the prettiest babe that e'er I nursed:
An I might live to see thee married once,
I have my wish.
    Lady Capulet. Marry, that 'marry' is the very theme
I came to talk of. Tell me, daughter Juliet,
How stands your dispositions to be married?
    Juliet. It is an honour that I dream not of.
    Nurse. An honour! Were not I thine only nurse,
I would say thou hadst sucked wisdom from thy teat.
70 *Lady Capulet.* Well, think of marriage now; younger
    than you
Here in Verona, ladies of esteem,
Are made already mothers. By my count,
I was your mother much upon these years
That you are now a maid. Thus then in brief:
The valiant Paris seeks you for his love.
    Nurse. A man, young lady! Lady, such a man
As all the world—Why, he's a man of wax.
    Lady Capulet. Verona's summer hath not such
    a flower.
    Nurse. Nay, he's a flower; in faith, a very flower.
80 *Lady Capulet.* What say you? Can you love
    the gentleman?
This night you shall behold him at our feast:
Read o'er the volume of young Paris' face,
And find delight writ there with beauty's pen;
Examine every married lineament,
And see how one another lends content;
And what obscured in this fair volume lies

Find written in the margent of his eyes.
This precious book of love, this unbound lover,
To beautify him, only lacks a cover.
The fish lives in the sea; and 'tis much pride   90
For fair without the fair within to hide.
That book in many's eyes doth share the glory,
That in gold clasps locks in the golden story:
So shall you share all that he doth possess,
By having him making yourself no less.
 Nurse. No less! Nay, bigger women grow by men!
 Lady Capulet. Speak briefly, can you like of
  Paris' love?
 Juliet. I'll look to like, if looking liking move;
But no more deep will I endart mine eye
Than your consent gives strength to make it fly.   100

   '*Enter Servingman*'

Servingman. Madam, the guests are come, supper
served up, you called, my young lady asked for, the
nurse cursed in the pantry, and everything in extremity.
I must hence to wait; I beseech you follow straight.
 Lady Capulet. We follow thee. Juliet, the
  County stays.
 Nurse. Go, girl, seek happy nights to happy days.
            [*they go*

[1. 4.]   *Without Capulet's house*

'*Enter* ROMEO, MERCUTIO, BENVOLIO, *with five or
six other masquers; torch-bearers*'

 Romeo. What, shall this speech be spoke for
  our excuse?
Or shall we on without apology?

Benvolio. The date is out of such prolixity:
We'll have no Cupid hoodwinked with a scarf,
Bearing a Tartar's painted bow of lath,
Scaring the ladies like a crow-keeper:
Nor no without-book prologue, faintly spoke
After the prompter, for our entrance:
But, let them measure us by what they will,
10 We'll measure them a measure and be gone.
    Romeo. Give me a torch: I am not for this ambling;
Being but heavy, I will bear the light.
    Mercutio. Nay, gentle Romeo, we must have
        you dance.
    Romeo. Not I, believe me: you have dancing shoes
With nimble soles; I have a soul of lead
So stakes me to the ground I cannot move.
    Mercutio. You are a lover: borrow Cupid's wings,
And soar with them above a common bound.
    Romeo. I am too sore enpiercéd with his shaft
20 To soar with his light feathers and so bound;
I cannot bound a pitch above dull woe:
Under love's heavy burden do I sink.
    Mercutio. And, to sink in it, should you
        burden love—
Too great oppression for a tender thing.
    Romeo. Is love a tender thing? It is too rough,
Too rude, too boisterous, and it pricks like thorn.
    Mercutio. If love be rough with you, be rough
        with love;
Prick love for pricking, and you beat love down.
Give me a case to put my visage in:
30 A visor for a visor! What care I
What curious eye doth quote deformities?
Here are the beetle-brows shall blush for me.
                        [*putting on a mask*

Benvolio. Come, knock and enter, and no sooner in
But every man betake him to his legs.

Romeo. A torch for me; let wantons light of heart
Tickle the senseless rushes with their heels.
For I am proverbed with a grandsire phrase,
I'll be a candle-holder, and look on.
The game was ne'er so fair, and I am done.

Mercutio. Tut, dun's the mouse, the constable's
   own word: 40
If thou art Dun, we'll draw thee from the mire,
Or save-your-reverence love, wherein thou stickest
Up to the ears. Come, we burn daylight, ho.

Romeo. Nay, that's not so.

Mercutio.   I mean, sir, in delay
We waste our lights in vain, like lights by day.
Take our good meaning, for our judgement sits
Five times in that ere once in our five wits.

Romeo. And we mean well in going to this masque,
But 'tis no wit to go.

Mercutio.   Why, may one ask?

Romeo. I dreamt a dream tonight.

Mercutio.   And so did I. 50

Romeo. Well, what was yours?

Mercutio.   That dreamers often lie.

Romeo. In bed asleep while they do dream things true.

Mercutio. O then I see Queen Mab hath been
   with you.
She is the fairies' midwife, and she comes
In shape no bigger than an agate-stone
On the fore-finger of an alderman,
Drawn with a team of little atomi
Over men's noses as they lie asleep.
Her chariot is an empty hazel-nut,
Made by the joiner squirrel or old grub   60

Time out o' mind the fairies' coachmakers:
Her waggon-spokes made of long spinners' legs,
The cover of the wings of grasshoppers,
Her traces of the smallest spider-web,
Her collars of the moonshine's watery beams,
Her whip of cricket's bone, the lash of film;
Her waggoner a small grey-coated gnat,
Not half so big as a round little worm
Pricked from the lazy finger of a maid.
70 And in this state she gallops night by night
Through lovers' brains, and then they dream of love;
O'er courtiers' knees, that dream on curtsies straight;
O'er lawyers' fingers who straight dream on fees;
O'er ladies' lips, who straight on kisses dream,
Which oft the angry Mab with blisters plagues
Because their breaths with sweetmeats tainted are.
Sometime she gallops o'er a courtier's nose,
And then dreams he of smelling out a suit:
And sometime comes she with a tithe-pig's tail
80 Tickling a parson's nose as 'a lies asleep,
Then dreams he of another benefice.
Sometime she driveth o'er a soldier's neck,
And then dreams he of cutting foreign throats,
Of breaches, ambuscadoes, Spanish blades,
Of healths five fathom deep; and then anon
Drums in his ear, at which he starts and wakes,
And being thus frighted swears a prayer or two,
And sleeps again. This is that very Mab
That plats the manes of horses in the night,
90 And bakes the elf-locks in foul sluttish hairs,
Which once untangled much misfortune bodes:
This is the hag, when maids lie on their backs,
That presses them and learns them first to bear,
Making them women of good carriage:

This is she—
Romeo.   Peace, peace, Mercutio, peace!
Thou talkst of nothing.
Mercutio.   True, I talk of dreams,
Which are the children of an idle brain,
Begot of nothing but vain fantasy,
Which is as thin of substance as the air,
And more inconstant than the wind, who woos   100
Even now the frozen bosom of the north,
And, being angered, puffs away from thence,
Turning his side to the dew-dropping south.
Benvolio. This wind you talk of blows us
    from ourselves:
Supper is done, and we shall come too late.
Romeo. I fear, too early: for my mind misgives
Some consequence, yet hanging in the stars,
Shall bitterly begin his fearful date
With this night's revels, and expire the term
Of a despiséd life closed in my breast,   110
By some vile forfeit of untimely death.
But He that hath the steerage of my course
Direct my sail! On, lusty gentlemen.
Benvolio. Strike, drum.   [*they march into the house*

[1. 5.]
*The hall in Capulet's house; musicians waiting. Enter
the masquers, march round the hall, and stand aside.
       'Servingmen come forth with napkins'*

First Servingman. Where's Potpan, that he helps not
to take away? He shift a trencher! He scrape a trencher!
Second Servingman. When good manners shall lie all
in one or two men's hands, and they unwashed too,
'tis a foul thing.

First Servingman. Away with the joined-stools, remove
the court-cupboard, look to the plate—Good thou,
save me a piece of marchpane; and, as thou loves me,
let the porter let in Susan Grindstone and Nell—
10 Antony and Potpan!

Third Servingman. Ay, boy, ready.

First Servingman. You are looked for and called for,
asked for and sought for, in the great chamber.

Fourth Servingman. We cannot be here and there too.
Cheerly, boys; be brisk a while, and the longer liver
take all.   [*Servingmen withdraw*

'*Enter*' CAPULET, *and* JULIET, *with* '*all the
guests and gentlewomen to the masquers*'

Capulet. Welcome, gentlemen! Ladies that have
their toes
Unplagued with corns will walk a bout with you.
Ah, my mistresses, which of you all
20 Will now deny to dance? She that makes dainty,
She I'll swear hath corns: am I come near ye now?
Welcome, gentlemen! I have seen the day
That I have worn a visor and could tell
A whispering tale in a fair lady's ear,
Such as would please: 'tis gone, 'tis gone, 'tis gone.
You are welcome, gentlemen! Come, musicians, play.
A hall, a hall! Give room. And foot it, girls.
                    ['*music plays and they dance*'
More light, you knaves, and turn the tables up,
And quench the fire—the room is grown too hot.
30 Ah, sirrah, this unlooked-for sport comes well.—
Nay sit, nay sit, good cousin Capulet,
For you and I are past our dancing days.
How long is't now since last yourself and I
Were in a masque?

Second Capulet.   By'r Lady, thirty years.

Capulet. What, man! 'tis not so much, 'tis not
 so much:
'Tis since the nuptial of Lucentio,
Come Pentecost as quickly as it will,
Some five and twenty years, and then we masqued.

Second Capulet. 'Tis more, 'tis more; his son is
 elder, sir:
His son is thirty.

Capulet.   Will you tell me that?   40
His son was but a ward two years ago.

Romeo. [*to a servingman*] What lady's that which doth
 enrich the hand
Of yonder knight?

Servingman.   I know not, sir.

(*Romeo.* O she doth teach the torches to burn bright!
It seems she hangs upon the cheek of night
As a rich jewel in an Ethiop's ear—
Beauty too rich for use, for earth too dear!
So shows a snowy dove trooping with crows,
As yonder lady o'er her fellows shows.
The measure done, I'll watch her place of stand,   50
And, touching hers, make blessèd my rude hand.
Did my heart love till now? Forswear it, sight!
For I ne'er saw true beauty till this night.

Tybalt. This, by his voice, should be a Montague.
Fetch me my rapier, boy. [*his page goes*] What dares
 the slave
Come hither, covered with an antic face,
To fleer and scorn at our solemnity?
Now, by the stock and honour of my kin,
To strike him dead I hold it not a sin.

Capulet. Why, how now, kinsman! wherefore storm
 you so?   60

Tybalt. Uncle, this is a Montague, our foe:
A villain that is hither come in spite,
To scorn at our solemnity this night.
  Capulet. Young Romeo is it?
  Tybalt.   'Tis he, that villain Romeo.
  Capulet. Content thee, gentle coz, let him alone,
'A bears him like a portly gentleman:
And, to say truth, Verona brags of him
To be a virtuous and well-governed youth.
I would not for the wealth of all this town
70 Here in my house do him disparagement:
Therefore be patient, take no note of him.
It is my will, the which if thou respect,
Show a fair presence and put off these frowns,
An ill-beseeming semblance for a feast.
  Tybalt. It fits when such a villain is a guest:
I'll not endure him.
  Capulet.   He shall be endured.
What, goodman boy? I say he shall. Go to,
Am I the master here, or you? Go to,
You'll not endure him? God shall mend my soul!
80 You'll make a mutiny among my guests!
You will set cock-a-hoop! You'll be the man!
  Tybalt. Why, uncle, 'tis a shame.
  Capulet.   Go to, go to,
You are a saucy boy. Is't so indeed?
This trick may chance to scathe you, I know what.
You must contrary me! Marry, 'tis time—
Well said, my hearts!—You are a princox: go,
Be quiet, or—More light, more light, for shame!—
I'll make you quiet.—What, cheerly, my hearts!
  Tybalt. Patience perforce with wilful
      choler meeting
90 Makes my flesh tremble in their different greeting.

I will withdraw, but this intrusion shall,
Now seeming sweet, convert to bitterest gall.   [*goes*

 Romeo. [*takes Juliet's hand*] If I profane with my
  unworthiest hand
This holy shrine, the gentle pain is this:
My lips, two blushing pilgrims, ready stand
To smooth that rough touch with a tender kiss.

 Juliet. Good pilgrim, you do wrong your hand
  too much,
Which mannerly devotion shows in this:
For saints have hands that pilgrims' hands do touch,
And palm to palm is holy palmers' kiss.   100

 Romeo. Have not saints lips, and holy palmers too?

 Juliet. Ay, pilgrim, lips that they must use
  in prayer.

 Romeo. O then, dear saint, let lips do what hands do,
They pray: grant thou, lest faith turn to despair.

 Juliet. Saints do not move, though grant for
  prayers' sake.

 Romeo. Then move not, while my prayer's effect
  I take.
Thus from my lips by thine my sin is purged.

            [*kissing her*

 Juliet. Then have my lips the sin that they
  have took.

 Romeo. Sin from my lips? O trespass sweetly urged!
Give me my sin again.   [*kissing her*

 Juliet.   You kiss by th' book. 110

 Nurse. Madam, your mother craves a word with you.

 Romeo. What is her mother?

 Nurse.   Marry, bachelor,
Her mother is the lady of the house,
And a good lady, and a wise and virtuous.
I nursed her daughter that you talked withal.

I tell you, he that can lay hold of her
Shall have the chinks.
 Romeo.   Is she a Capulet?
O dear account! My life is my foe's debt.
 Benvolio. Away be gone; the sport is at the best.
120 *Romeo.* Ay, so I fear; the more is my unrest.
 Capulet. Nay, gentlemen, prepare not to be gone;
We have a trifling foolish banquet towards.

 The masquers excuse themselves, whispering in his ear

Is it e'en so? Why, then, I thank you all:
I thank you, honest gentlemen; good night.
More torches here; come on! then let's to bed.

  Servants bring torches to escort the masquers out

Ah, sirrah, by my fay, it waxes late:
I'll to my rest.   *[all leave but Juliet and Nurse*
 Juliet. Come hither, nurse. What is yond gentleman?
 Nurse. The son and heir of old Tiberio.
130 *Juliet.* What's he that now is going out of door?
 Nurse. Marry, that I think be young Petruchio.
 Juliet. What's he that follows there, that would
  not dance?
 Nurse. I know not.
 Juliet. Go ask his name.—If he be marriéd,
My grave is like to be my wedding bed.
 Nurse. His name is Romeo, and a Montague,
The only son of your great enemy.
 (*Juliet.* My only love sprung from my only hate!
Too early seen unknown, and known too late!
140 Prodigious birth of love it is to me,
That I must love a loathéd enemy.
 Nurse. What's this, what's this?
 Juliet.   A rhyme I learned even now
Of one I danced withal.

'One calls within, "Juliet"'

Nurse.   Anon, anon!
Come, let's away; the strangers all are gone.

                                   [*they go*

[2. *Prologue*]

Enter Chorus

Chorus. Now old desire doth in his deathbed lie,
   And young affection gapes to be his heir;
That fair for which love groaned for and would die,
   With tender Juliet matched, is now not fair.
Now Romeo is beloved and loves again,
   Alike bewitchéd by the charm of looks,
But to his foe supposed he must complain,
   And she steal love's sweet bait from fearful hooks:
Being held a foe, he may not have access
   To breathe such vows as lovers use to swear;   10
And she as much in love, her means much less
   To meet her new belovéd anywhere:
But passion lends them power, time means, to meet,
Tempering extremities with extreme sweet.   [*exit*

[2. 1.]
*Capulet's orchard; to the one side the outer wall with a
lane beyond, to the other Capulet's house showing an
upper window*

   'Enter ROMEO alone' in the lane

 Romeo. Can I go forward when my heart is here?
Turn back, dull earth, and find thy centre out.
   [*he climbs the wall and leaps into the orchard*

'Enter BENVOLIO with MERCUTIO' in the lane.
Romeo listens behind the wall

Benvolio.   Romeo, my cousin Romeo!
Mercutio.   He is wise,
And on my life hath stolen him home to bed.
    Benvolio.   He ran this way and leapt this
      orchard wall.
Call, good Mercutio.
    Mercutio.   Nay, I'll conjure too.
Romeo, humours, madman, passion, lover!
Appear thou in the likeness of a sigh;
Speak but one rhyme and I am satisfied:
10 Cry but 'Ay me!', pronounce but 'love' and 'dove';
Speak to my gossip Venus one fair word,
One nickname for her purblind son and heir,
Young Abraham Cupid, he that shot so trim
When King Cophetua loved the beggar maid.
He heareth not, he stirreth not, he moveth not;
The ape is dead, and I must conjure him.
I conjure thee by Rosaline's bright eyes,
By her high forehead and her scarlet lip,
By her fine foot, straight leg, and quivering thigh,
20 And the demesnes that there adjacent lie,
That in thy likeness thou appear to us.
    Benvolio.   An if he hear thee, thou wilt anger him.
    Mercutio.   This cannot anger him. 'Twould
      anger him
To raise a spirit in his mistress' circle
Of some strange nature, letting it there stand
Till she had laid it and conjured it down;
That were some spite. My invocation
Is fair and honest; in his mistress' name
I conjure only but to raise up him.

Benvolio. Come! He hath hid himself among
    these trees   30
To be consorted with the humorous night:
Blind is his love and best befits the dark.
  Mercutio. If love be blind, love cannot hit the mark.
Now will he sit under a medlar tree,
And wish his mistress were that kind of fruit
As maids call medlars when they laugh alone.
O Romeo, that she were, O that she were
An open-arse and thou a poperin pear!
Romeo, goodnight. I'll to my truckle-bed;
This field-bed is too cold for me to sleep.   40
Come, shall we go?
  Benvolio.   Go then, for 'tis in vain
To seek him here that means not to be found.

                               [they go
[2. 2.] *Romeo.* He jests at scars that never felt a wound.

JULIET appears aloft at the window

But soft! What light through yonder window breaks?
It is the east, and Juliet is the sun.
Arise, fair sun, and kill the envious moon,
Who is already sick and pale with grief
That thou, her maid, art far more fair than she.
Be not her maid, since she is envious.
Her vestal livery is but sick and green,
And none but fools do wear it: cast it off.
It is my lady, O it is my love;   10
O that she knew she were.
She speaks, yet she says nothing. What of that?
Her eye discourses: I will answer it.
I am too bold: 'tis not to me she speaks.
Two of the fairest stars in all the heaven,
Having some business, do entreat her eyes

To twinkle in their spheres till they return.
What if her eyes were there, they in her head?
The brightness of her cheek would shame those stars
20 As daylight doth a lamp; her eyes in heaven
Would through the airy region stream so bright
That birds would sing and think it were not night.
See how she leans her cheek upon her hand!
O that I were a glove upon that hand,
That I might touch that cheek.
    Juliet.   Ay me!
    (*Romeo.*   She speaks.
O speak again, bright angel, for thou art
As glorious to this night, being o'er my head,
As is a wingéd messenger of heaven
Unto the white-upturnéd wondering eyes
30 Of mortals that fall back to gaze on him
When he bestrides the lazy-passing clouds
And sails upon the bosom of the air.
    Juliet. O Romeo, Romeo! Wherefore art
        thou Romeo?
Deny thy father and refuse thy name:
Or, if thou wilt not, be but sworn my love,
And I'll no longer be a Capulet.
    (*Romeo.* Shall I hear more, or shall I speak at this?
    Juliet. 'Tis but thy name that is my enemy.
Thou art thy self, though not a Montague.
40 O be some other name! What's Montague?
It is nor hand, nor foot, nor arm, nor face,
Nor any part belonging to a man.
What's in a name? That which we call a rose
By any other name would smell as sweet.
So Romeo would, were he not Romeo called,
Retain that dear perfection which he owes,
Without that title. Romeo, doff thy name;

And for thy name, which is no part of thee,
Take all myself.
   Romeo.   I take thee at thy word.
Call me but love, and I'll be new baptized;   50
Henceforth I never will be Romeo.
   Juliet. What man art thou that, thus bescreened
     in night,
So stumblest on my counsel?
   Romeo.   By a name
I know not how to tell thee who I am.
My name, dear saint, is hateful to myself
Because it is an enemy to thee.
Had I it written, I would tear the word.
   Juliet. My ears have yet not drunk a
     hundred words
Of thy tongue's uttering, yet I know the sound.
Art thou not Romeo, and a Montague?   60
   Romeo. Neither, fair maid, if either thee dislike.
   Juliet. How camest thou hither, tell me,
     and wherefore?
The orchard walls are high and hard to climb,
And the place death, considering who thou art,
If any of my kinsmen find thee here.
   Romeo. With love's light wings did I o'erperch
     these walls;
For stony limits cannot hold love out,
And what love can do, that dares love attempt:
Therefore thy kinsmen are no stop to me.
   Juliet. If they do see thee, they will murther thee.   70
   Romeo. Alack, there lies more peril in thine eye
Than twenty of their swords. Look thou but sweet,
And I am proof against their enmity.
   Juliet. I would not for the world they saw
     thee here.

Romeo. I have night's cloak to hide me from
    their eyes;
And but thou love me, let them find me here:
My life were better ended by their hate
Than death proroguéd, wanting of thy love.
  Juliet. By whose direction foundst thou out
    this place?
80 *Romeo.* By love, that first did prompt me to enquire.
He lent me counsel, and I lent him eyes.
I am no pilot; yet, wert thou as far
As that vast shore washed with the farthest sea,
I should adventure for such merchandise.
  Juliet. Thou knowest the mask of night is on
    my face;
Else would a maiden blush bepaint my cheek,
For that which thou hast heard me speak tonight.
Fain would I dwell on form; fain, fain deny
What I have spoke: but farewell compliment!
90 Dost thou love me? I know thou wilt say 'Ay',
And I will take thy word. Yet, if thou swearst,
Thou mayst prove false. At lovers' perjuries
They say Jove laughs. O gentle Romeo,
If thou dost love, pronounce it faithfully.
Or, if thou think'st I am too quickly won,
I'll frown and be perverse and say thee nay,
So thou wilt woo; but else, not for the world.
In truth, fair Montague, I am too fond,
And therefore thou mayst think my haviour light;
100 But trust me, gentleman, I'll prove more true
Than those that have more cunning to be strange.
I should have been more strange, I must confess,
But that thou overheardst, ere I was ware,
My true-love passion. Therefore pardon me,
And not impute this yielding to light love,

Which the dark night hath so discoveréd.

Romeo. Lady, by yonder blesséd moon I vow,
That tips with silver all these fruit tree tops—

   Juliet. O swear not by the moon, th'incon-
     stant moon,
That monthly changes in her circled orb,   110
Lest that thy love prove likewise variable.

   Romeo. What shall I swear by?

   Juliet.   Do not swear at all:
Or, if thou wilt, swear by thy gracious self,
Which is the god of my idolatry,
And I'll believe thee.

   Romeo.   If my heart's dear love—

   Juliet. Well, do not swear. Although I joy in thee,
I have no joy of this contract tonight:
It is too rash, too unadvised, too sudden,
Too like the lightning, which doth cease to be
Ere one can say 'It lightens'. Sweet, goodnight: 120
This bud of love, by summer's ripening breath,
May prove a beauteous flower when next we meet.
Goodnight, goodnight! As sweet repose and rest
Come to thy heart as that within my breast.

   Romeo. O wilt thou leave me so unsatisfied?

   Juliet. What satisfaction canst thou have tonight?

   Romeo. Th'exchange of thy love's faithful vow
     for mine.

   Juliet. I gave thee mine before thou didst
     request it:
And yet I would it were to give again.

   Romeo. Would'st thou withdraw it? For what
     purpose, love?   130

   Juliet. But to be frank and give it thee again:
And yet I wish but for the thing I have.
My bounty is as boundless as the sea,

My love as deep: the more I give to thee,
The more I have: for both are infinite.
I hear some noise within. Dear love, adieu—

       [Nurse calls within

Anon, good nurse!—sweet Montague, be true.
Stay but a little; I will come again.   *[Juliet goes in*
 Romeo. O blessed, blessed night! I am afeared,
140 Being in night, all this is but a dream,
Too flattering sweet to be substantial.

    JULIET reappears at the window

 Juliet. Three words, dear Romeo, and good
    night indeed.
If that thy bent of love be honourable,
Thy purpose marriage, send me word tomorrow,
By one that I'll procure to come to thee,
Where and what time thou wilt perform the rite;
And all my fortunes at thy foot I'll lay,
And follow thee my lord throughout the world.
 Nurse. [*within*] Madam!
150 *Juliet.* I come, anon.—But if thou meanest not well,
I do beseech thee—
 Nurse. [*within*]   Madam!
 Juliet.   By and by I come—
To cease thy suit, and leave me to my grief.
Tomorrow will I send.
 Romeo. So thrive my soul—
 Juliet.   A thousand times good night!

            [she goes in

 Romeo. A thousand times the worse, to want
    thy light!
Love goes toward love as schoolboys from
    their books,
But love from love, toward school with heavy looks.

JULIET returns to the window

Juliet. Hist, Romeo, hist! O for a falconer's voice
To lure this tassel-gentle back again!
Bondage is hoarse and may not speak aloud,   160
Else would I tear the cave where Echo lies,
And make her airy tongue more hoarse than mine
With repetition of my "Romeo!"
Romeo. It is my soul that calls upon my name.
How silver-sweet sound lovers' tongues by night,
Like softest music to attending ears!
Juliet. Romeo!
Romeo.   My niëss!
Juliet.   What o'clock tomorrow
Shall I send to thee?
Romeo.   By the hour of nine.
Juliet. I will not fail. 'Tis twenty year till then.
I have forgot why I did call thee back.   170
Romeo. Let me stand here till thou remember it.
Juliet. I shall forget, to have thee still stand there,
Rememb'ring how I love thy company.
Romeo. And I'll still stay, to have thee still forget,
Forgetting any other home but this.
Juliet. 'Tis almost morning. I would have
      thee gone,
And yet no farther than a wanton's bird,
That lets it hop a little from her hand,
Like a poor prisoner in his twisted gyves,
And with a silk thread plucks it back again,   180
So loving-jealous of his liberty.
Romeo. I would I were thy bird.
Juliet.   Sweet, so would I;
Yet I should kill thee with much cherishing.
Goodnight, goodnight! Parting is such sweet sorrow,

That I shall say goodnight till it be morrow.
  Romeo. Sleep dwell upon thine eyes, peace in
    thy breast!
Would I were sleep and peace, so sweet to rest!

                                [she goes in

Hence will I to my ghostly sire's close cell,
His help to crave, and my dear hap to tell.   *[he goes*

[2. 3.]   *Friar Lawrence's cell*

          '*Enter* FRIAR *alone with a basket*'

  Friar. The grey-eyed morn smiles on the
    frowning night,
Check'ring the eastern clouds with streaks of light:
And darkness fleck'd like a drunkard reels
From forth day's pathway, made by Titan's wheels:
Now ere the sun advance his burning eye,
The day to cheer and night's dank dew to dry,
I must upfill this osier cage of ours,
With baleful weeds and precious-juicéd flowers.
The earth that's nature's mother is her tomb;
10 What is her burying grave, that is her womb;
And from her womb children of divers kind
We sucking on her natural bosom find:
Many for many virtues excellent,
None but for some, and yet all different.
O mickle is the powerful grace that lies
In plants, herbs, stones, and their true qualities:
For nought so vile that on the earth doth live
But to the earth some special good doth give:
Nor aught so good but, strained from that
    fair use,
20 Revolts from true birth, stumbling on abuse.

Virtue itself turns vice, being misapplied,
And vice sometime by action dignified.

ROMEO approaches, unseen by the Friar

Within the infant rind of this weak flower
Poison hath residence, and medicine power:
For this, being smelt, with that part cheers each part;
Being tasted, stays all senses with the heart.
Two such opposéd kings encamp them still
In man as well as herbs—grace and rude will:
And where the worser is predominant,
Full soon the canker death eats up that plant.   30
  Romeo. Good morrow, father.
  Friar.   Benedicite!
What early tongue so sweet saluteth me?
Young son, it argues a distempered head,
So soon to bid goodmorrow to thy bed.
Care keeps his watch in every old man's eye,
And where care lodges sleep will never lie:
But where unbruiséd youth with unstuffed brain
Doth couch his limbs, there golden sleep doth reign.
Therefore thy earliness doth me assure
Thou art uproused with some distemperature: 40
Or if not so, then here I hit it right—
Our Romeo hath not been in bed tonight.
  Romeo. That last is true—the sweeter rest was mine.
  Friar. God pardon sin! Wast thou with Rosaline?
  Romeo. With Rosaline? My ghostly father, no;
I have forgot that name, and that name's woe.
  Friar. That's my good son! But where hast thou
      been then?
  Romeo. I'll tell thee ere thou ask it me again.
I have been feasting with mine enemy,
Where on a sudden one hath wounded me   50

That's by me wounded. Both our remedies
Within thy help and holy physic lies.
I bear no hatred, blessed man, for lo,
My intercession likewise steads my foe.

  Friar. Be plain, good son, and homely in thy drift.
Riddling confession finds but riddling shrift.

  Romeo. Then plainly know my heart's dear love
     is set
On the fair daughter of rich Capulet:
As mine on hers, so hers is set on mine,

60 And all combined save what thou must combine
By holy marriage: when and where and how
We met, we wooed, and made exchange of vow
I'll tell thee as we pass; but this I pray,
That thou consent to marry us today.

  Friar. Holy Saint Francis, what a change is here!
Is Rosaline, that thou didst love so dear,
So soon forsaken? Young men's love then lies
Not truly in their hearts but in their eyes.
Jesu Maria, what a deal of brine

70 Hath washed thy sallow cheeks for Rosaline!
How much salt water thrown away in waste
To season love, that of it doth not taste!
The sun not yet thy sighs from heaven clears,
Thy old groans ring yet in mine ancient ears;
Lo, here upon thy cheek the stain doth sit
Of an old tear that is not washed off yet.
If e'er thou wast thyself, and these woes thine,
Thou and these woes were all for Rosaline.
And art thou changed? Pronounce this sentence, then—

80 Women may fall, when there's no strength in men.

  Romeo. Thou chid'st me oft for loving Rosaline.

  Friar. For doting, not for loving, pupil mine.

  Romeo. And bad'st me bury love.

Friar.   Not in a grave
To lay one in, another out to have.
Romeo. I pray thee chide me not. Her I love now
Doth grace for grace and love for love allow:
The other did not so.
Friar.   O, she knew well
Thy love did read by rote, that could not spell.
But come, young waverer, come go with me;
In one respect I'll thy assistant be: 90
For this alliance may so happy prove
To turn your households' rancour to pure love.
Romeo. O let us hence! I stand on sudden haste.
Friar. Wisely and slow. They stumble that run fast.

[*they go*

[2. 4.]   *A public place*

'*Enter* BENVOLIO *and* MERCUTIO'

Mercutio. Where the devil should this Romeo be?
Came he not home tonight?
Benvolio. Not to his father's; I spoke with his man.
Mercutio. Why, that same pale hard-hearted wench,
    that Rosaline,
Torments him so, that he will sure run mad.
Benvolio. Tybalt, the kinsman to old Capulet,
Hath sent a letter to his father's house.
Mercutio. A challenge, on my life.
Benvolio. Romeo will answer it.
Mercutio. Any man that can write may answer a letter. 10
Benvolio. Nay, he will answer the letter's master, how
he dares being dared.
Mercutio. Alas, poor Romeo, he is already dead—
stabbed with a white wench's black eye, run through
the ear with a love-song, the very pin of his heart

cleft with the blind bow-boy's butt-shaft; and is he a
man to encounter Tybalt?

Benvolio. Why, what is Tybalt?

Mercutio. More than Prince of Cats. O, he's the
20 courageous captain of compliments. He fights as you
sing pricksong—keeps time, distance, and proportion; he
rests his minim rests—one, two, and the third in your
bosom. The very butcher of a silk button, a duellist, a
duellist, a gentleman of the very first house, of the first
and second cause! Ah, the immortal passado, the punto
reverso, the hai!

Benvolio. The what?

Mercutio. The pox of such antic, lisping, affecting
fantasticoes, these new tuners of accent! 'By Jesu, a
30 very good blade! a very tall man! a very good whore!'
Why, is not this a lamentable thing, grandsire, that we
should be thus afflicted with these strange flies, these
fashion-mongers, these pardon-me's, who stand so much
on the new form that they cannot sit at ease on the old
bench? O, their bones, their bones!

'Enter ROMEO'

Benvolio. Here comes Romeo, here comes Romeo!

Mercutio. Without his roe, like a dried herring. O
flesh, flesh, how art thou fishified! Now is he for the
numbers that Petrarch flowed in. Laura to his lady
40 was a kitchen wench—marry, she had a better love to
be-rhyme her!—Dido a dowdy, Cleopatra a gipsy,
Helen and Hero hildings and harlots, Thisbe a gray
eye or so, but not to the purpose. Signior Romeo, bon
jour! There's a French salutation to your French slop.
You gave us the counterfeit fairly last night.

Romeo. Good morrow to you both. What counterfeit
did I give you?

Mercutio. The slip, sir, the slip. Can you not conceive?

Romeo. Pardon, good Mercutio. My business was great, and in such a case as mine a man may strain courtesy. 50

Mercutio. That's as much as to say, such a case as yours constrains a man to bow in the hams.

Romeo. Meaning to curtsy?

Mercutio. Thou hast most kindly hit it.

Romeo. A most courteous exposition.

Mercutio. Nay, I am the very pink of courtesy.

Romeo. Pink for flower?

Mercutio. Right.

Romeo. Why, then is my pump well flowered. 60

Mercutio. Sure wit! Follow me this jest now till thou hast worn out thy pump, that, when the single sole of it is worn, the jest may remain, after the wearing, solely singular.

Romeo. O single-soled jest, solely singular for the singleness!

Mercutio. Come between us, good Benvolio; my wits faints.

Romeo. Switch and spurs, switch and spurs; or I'll cry a match. 70

Mercutio. Nay, if our wits run the wild-goose chase, I am done: for thou hast more of the wild goose in one of thy wits than, I am sure, I have in my whole five. Was I with you there for the goose?

Romeo. Thou wast never with me for anything when thou wast not there for the goose.

Mercutio. I will bite thee by the ear for that jest.

Romeo. Nay, good goose, bite not.

Mercutio. Thy wit is a very bitter sweeting; it is a most sharp sauce. 80

Romeo. And is it not then well served in to a sweet goose?

Mercutio. O, here's a wit of cheveril, that stretches from an inch narrow to an ell broad.

Romeo. I stretch it out for that word 'broad', which, added to the goose, proves thee far and wide a broad goose.

Mercutio. Why, is not this better now than groaning for love? Now art thou sociable, now art thou Romeo: now art thou what thou art, by art as well as by nature. For this drivelling love is like a great natural that runs

90 lolling up and down to hide his bauble in a hole.

Benvolio. Stop there, stop there!

Mercutio. Thou desirest me to stop in my tale, against the hair?

Benvolio. Thou wouldst else have made thy tale large.

Mercutio. O, thou art deceived! I would have made it short, for I was come to the whole depth of my tale, and meant indeed to occupy the argument no longer.

*The NURSE in her best array is seen
approaching with her man PETER*

Romeo. Here's goodly gear! A sail, a sail!

Mercutio. Two, two! a shirt and a smock.

100 *Nurse.* Peter!

Peter. Anon.

Nurse. My fan, Peter.

(*Mercutio.* Good Peter, to hide her face; for her fan's the fairer face.

Nurse. God ye good morrow, gentlemen.

Mercutio. God ye good-den, fair gentlewoman.

Nurse. Is it good-den?

Mercutio. 'Tis no less, I tell ye; for the bawdy hand of the dial is now upon the prick of noon.

110 *Nurse.* Out upon you! What a man are you?

Romeo. One, gentlewoman, that God hath made, himself to mar.

Nurse. By my troth, it is well said. 'For himself to mar,' quoth 'a? Gentlemen, can any of you tell me where I may find the young Romeo?

Romeo. I can tell you; but young Romeo will be older when you have found him than he was when you sought him. I am the youngest of that name, for fault of a worse.

Nurse. You say well.

Mercutio. Yea, is the worst well? Very well took, 120 i' faith! Wisely, wisely!

Nurse. If you be he, sir, I desire some confidence with you.

Benvolio. She will indite him to some supper.

(*Mercutio.* A bawd, a bawd, a bawd! So ho!

Romeo. What, hast thou found?

Mercutio. No hare, sir; unless a hare, sir, in a lenten pie, that is something stale and hoar ere it be spent.

'He walks by them and sings'

> An old hare hoar
> And an old hare hoar
> Is very good meat in Lent.   130
> But a hare that is hoar
> Is too much for a score
> When it hoars ere it be spent.

Romeo, will you come to your father's? We'll to dinner thither.

Romeo. I will follow you.

Mercutio. Farewell, ancient lady; farewell, [*singing*] 'lady, lady, lady'.   [*Mercutio and Benvolio go off*

Nurse. I pray you, sir, what saucy merchant was this 140 that was so full of his ropery?

Romeo. A gentleman, Nurse, that loves to hear himself talk, and will speak more in a minute than he will stand to in a month.

Nurse. And 'a speak anything against me, I'll take
him down and 'a were lustier than he is, and twenty
such Jacks: and if I cannot, I'll find those that shall.
Scurvy knave! I am none of his flirt-gills, I am none of
his skains-mates. [*To Peter*] And thou must stand by
150 too, and suffer every knave to use me at his pleasure!

Peter. I saw no man use you at his pleasure. If I had,
my weapon should quickly have been out. I warrant
you I dare draw as soon as another man, if I see occasion
in a good quarrel, and the law on my side.

Nurse. Now afore God, I am so vexed that every part
about me quivers. Scurvy knave! Pray you, sir, a word.
And as I told you, my young lady bid me enquire you
out. What she bid me say I will keep to myself: but first
let me tell ye, if ye should lead her in a fool's paradise,
160 as they say, it were a very gross kind of behaviour, as
they say: for the gentlewoman is young; and therefore,
if you should deal double with her, truly it were an ill
thing to be offered to any gentlewoman, and very weak
dealing.

Romeo. Nurse, commend me to thy lady and mistress.
I protest unto thee—

Nurse. Good heart! and i' faith I will tell her as much.
Lord, Lord! she will be a joyful woman.

Romeo. What wilt thou tell her, Nurse? Thou dost not
170 mark me!

Nurse. I will tell her, sir, that you do protest, which,
as I take it, is a gentlemanlike offer.

Romeo. Bid her devise
Some means to come to shrift this afternoon,
And there she shall at Friar Lawrence' cell
Be shrived and married. Here is for thy pains.

Nurse. No, truly, sir; not a penny.

Romeo Go to, I say you shall.

Nurse. This afternoon, sir; well, she shall be there.

Romeo. And stay, good Nurse, behind the abbey wall. 180
Within this hour my man shall be with thee
And bring thee cords made like a tackled stair,
Which to the high topgallant of my joy
Must be my convoy in the secret night.
Farewell. Be trusty, and I'll quit thy pains.
Farewell. Commend me to thy mistress.

Nurse. Now God in heaven bless thee! Hark you, sir.

Romeo. What sayst thou, my dear Nurse?

Nurse. Is your man secret? Did you ne'er hear say,
'Two may keep counsel, putting one away'?   190

Romeo. I warrant thee my man's as true as steel.

Nurse. Well, sir, my mistress is the sweetest lady.
Lord, Lord! when 'twas a little prating thing—O, there
is a nobleman in town, one Paris, that would fain lay
knife aboard: but she, good soul, had as lief see a toad,
a very toad, as see him. I anger her sometimes, and
tell her that Paris is the properer man; but I'll warrant
you, when I say so, she looks as pale as any clout in the
versal world. Doth not rosemary and Romeo begin both
with a letter?   200

Romeo. Ay, Nurse; what of that? Both with an R.

Nurse. Ah, mocker, that's the dog-name; R is for
the—No; I know it begins with some other letter; and
she hath the prettiest sententious of it, of you and
rosemary, that it would do you good to hear it.

Romeo. Commend me to thy lady.

Nurse. Ay, a thousand times. [*Romeo goes*] Peter!

Peter. Anon.

Nurse. Before and apace.   [*they go*

Capulet's orchard

'*Enter* JULIET'

Juliet. The clock struck nine when I did send
    the Nurse;
In half an hour she promised to return.
Perchance she cannot meet him. That's not so.
O, she is lame! Love's heralds should be thoughts,
Which ten times faster glides than the sun's beams
Driving back shadows over louring hills.
Therefore do nimble-pinioned doves draw Love,
And therefore hath the wind-swift Cupid wings.
Now is the sun upon the highmost hill
10 Of this day's journey, and from nine till twelve
Is three long hours; yet she is not come.
Had she affections and warm youthful blood,
She would be swift in motion as a ball;
My words would bandy her to my sweet love,
And his to me.
But old folks, many feign as they were dead—
Unwieldy, slow, heavy, and pale as lead.

'*Enter* NURSE', *with* PETER

O God, she comes! O honey Nurse, what news?
Hast thou met with him? Send thy man away.
20 *Nurse.* Peter, stay at the gate.   [*Peter withdraws*
    Juliet. Now good sweet Nurse—O Lord, why
    look'st thou sad?
Though news be sad, yet tell them merrily;
If good, thou shamest the music of sweet news
By playing it to me with so sour a face.
    Nurse. I am aweary, give me leave a while.
Fie, how my bones ache! What a jaunce have I!

Juliet. I would thou hadst my bones, and I
    thy news:
Nay, come, I pray thee speak; good, good
    Nurse, speak.
Nurse. Jesu, what haste! Can you not stay awhile?
Do you not see that I am out of breath?   30
  Juliet. How art thou out of breath when thou
    hast breath
To say to me that thou art out of breath?
The excuse that thou dost make in this delay
Is longer than the tale thou dost excuse.
Is thy news good or bad? Answer to that.
Say either, and I'll stay the circumstance.
Let me be satisfied; is't good or bad?
  Nurse. Well, you have made a simple choice; you
know not how to choose a man. Romeo? No, not he.
Though his face be better than any man's, yet his leg 40
excels all men's; and for a hand and a foot and a body,
though they be not to be talked on, yet they are past
compare. He is not the flower of courtesy, but, I'll
warrant him, as gentle as a lamb. Go thy ways, wench;
serve God. What, have you dined at home?
  Juliet. No, no. But all this did I know before.
What says he of our marriage, what of that?
  Nurse. Lord, how my head aches! what a head have I!
It beats as it would fall in twenty pieces.
My back o' t'other side; ah, my back, my back! 50
Beshrew your heart for sending me about
To catch my death with jauncing up and down.
  Juliet. I' faith, I am sorry that thou art not well.
Sweet, sweet, sweet Nurse, tell me, what says my love?
  Nurse. Your love says, like an honest gentleman, and a
courteous, and a kind, and a handsome, and, I warrant,
a virtuous—Where is your mother?

Juliet. Where is my mother? Why, she is within.
Where should she be? How oddly thou repliest:
60 'Your love says, like an honest gentleman,
"Where is your mother?"'
  Nurse.   O God's Lady dear!
Are you so hot? Marry come up, I trow!
Is this the poultice for my aching bones?
Henceforward do your messages yourself.
  Juliet. Here's such a coil! Come, what says Romeo?
  Nurse. Have you got leave to go to shrift today?
  Juliet. I have.
  Nurse. Then hie you hence to Friar Lawrence' cell;
There stays a husband to make you a wife.
70 Now comes the wanton blood up in your cheeks;
They'll be in scarlet straight at any news.
Hie you to church; I must another way,
To fetch a ladder, by the which your love
Must climb a bird's nest soon when it is dark.
I am the drudge, and toil in your delight:
But you shall bear the burden soon at night.
Go; I'll to dinner; hie you to the cell.
  Juliet. Hie to high fortune! Honest Nurse, farewell.
                                          [*they go*

[2. 6.]   *Friar Lawrence's cell*

'*Enter* FRIAR *and* ROMEO'

  Friar. So smile the heavens upon this holy act
That after-hours with sorrow chide us not.
  Romeo. Amen, amen. But come what sorrow can,
It cannot countervail the exchange of joy
That one short minute gives me in her sight.
Do thou but close our hands with holy words,

Then love-devouring death do what he dare;
It is enough I may but call her mine.
  Friar. These violent delights have violent ends,
And in their triumph die like fire and powder   10
Which, as they kiss, consume. The sweetest honey
Is loathsome in his own deliciousness,
And in the taste confounds the appetite.
Therefore love moderately; long love doth so:
Too swift arrives as tardy as too slow.
Here comes the lady.

'*Enter* JULIET'

O, so light a foot

Will ne'er wear out the everlasting flint!
A lover may bestride the gossamers
That idles in the wanton summer air,
And yet not fall; so light is vanity.   20
  Juliet. Good even to my ghostly confessor.
  Friar. Romeo shall thank thee, daughter, for
    us both.
  Juliet. As much to him, else is his thanks too much.

[*they embrace*

  Romeo. Ah, Juliet, if the measure of thy joy
Be heaped like mine, and that thy skill be more
To blazon it, then sweeten with thy breath
This neighbour air, and let rich music's tongue
Unfold the imagined happiness that both
Receive in either by this dear encounter.
  Juliet. Conceit, more rich in matter than
    in words,   30
Brags of his substance, not of ornament.
They are but beggars that can count their worth;
But my true love is grown to such excess
I cannot sum up sum of half my wealth.

Friar. Come, come with me, and we will make
    short work;
For, by your leaves, you shall not stay alone
Till Holy Church incorporate two in one.   [*they go*

[3. 1.]   *A public place*

'*Enter* MERCUTIO, BENVOLIO, *and*' *their* '*men*'

Benvolio. I pray thee, good Mercutio, let's retire;
The day is hot, the Capels are abroad:
And if we meet we shall not scape a brawl,
For now, these hot days, is the mad blood stirring.

Mercutio. Thou art like one of these fellows that, when
he enters the confines of a tavern, claps me his sword
upon the table and says 'God send me no need of thee';
and, by the operation of the second cup, draws him on
the drawer, when indeed there is no need.

10 *Benvolio.* Am I like such a fellow?

Mercutio. Come, come, thou art as hot a Jack in thy
mood as any in Italy; and as soon moved to be moody,
and as soon moody to be moved.

Benvolio. And what to?

Mercutio. Nay, an there were two such, we should
have none shortly, for one would kill the other. Thou?
Why, thou wilt quarrel with a man that hath a hair
more or a hair less in his beard than thou hast. Thou
wilt quarrel with a man for cracking nuts, having no
20 other reason but because thou hast hazel eyes. What
eye but such an eye would spy out such a quarrel? Thy
head is as full of quarrels as an egg is full of meat, and
yet thy head hath been beaten as addle as an egg for
quarrelling. Thou hast quarrelled with a man for

coughing in the street, because he hath wakened thy
dog that hath lain asleep in the sun. Didst thou not fall
out with a tailor for wearing his new doublet before
Easter? With another for tying his new shoes with old
riband? And yet thou wilt tutor me from quarrelling?

Benvolio. An I were so apt to quarrel as thou art, 30
any man should buy the fee-simple of my life for an
hour and a quarter.

Mercutio. The fee-simple? O simple!

'*Enter* TYBALT,' '*and others*'

Benvolio. By my head, here comes the Capulets.

Mercutio. By my heel, I care not.

Tybalt. Follow me close, for I will speak to them.
Gentlemen, good-den: a word with one of you.

Mercutio. And but one word with one of us? Couple
it with something; make it a word and a blow.

Tybalt. You shall find me apt enough to that, sir, an 40
you will give me occasion.

Mercutio. Could you not take some occasion without
giving?

Tybalt. Mercutio, thou consort'st with Romeo—

Mercutio. Consort? What, dost thou make us minstrels? An thou make minstrels of us, look to hear
nothing but discords. Here's my fiddlestick; here's that
shall make you dance. Zounds, consort!

Benvolio. We talk here in the public haunt
        of men.
Either withdraw unto some private place   50
And reason coldly of your grievances,
Or else depart: here all eyes gaze on us.

Mercutio. Men's eyes were made to look, and let
        them gaze.
I will not budge for no man's pleasure, I.

'*Enter* ROMEO'

Tybalt. Well, peace be with you, sir; here comes
  my man.
Mercutio. But I'll be hanged, sir, if he wears
  your livery.
Marry, go before to field, he'll be your follower!
Your worship in that sense may call him man.
Tybalt. Romeo, the love I bear thee can afford
60 No better term than this: thou art a villain.
  Romeo. Tybalt, the reason that I have to love thee
Doth much excuse the appertaining rage
To such a greeting. Villain am I none—
Therefore farewell; I see thou knowest me not.
  Tybalt. Boy, this shall not excuse the injuries
That thou hast done me; therefore turn and draw.
  Romeo. I do protest I never injured thee,
But love thee better than thou canst devise
Till thou shalt know the reason of my love:
70 And so, good Capulet, which name I tender
As dearly as mine own, be satisfied.
  Mercutio. O calm, dishonourable, vile submission!
'Alla stoccata' carries it away.   [*draws*
Tybalt, you rat-catcher, will you walk?
  Tybalt. What wouldst thou have with me?
  Mercutio. Good King of Cats, nothing but one of
your nine lives that I mean to make bold withal and,
as you shall use me hereafter, dry-beat the rest of the
eight. Will you pluck your sword out of his pilcher by
80 the ears? Make haste, lest mine be about your ears ere
it be out.
  Tybalt. I am for you.   [*draws*
  Romeo. Gentle Mercutio, put thy rapier up.
  Mercutio. Come, sir, your passado.   [*they fight*

Romeo. Draw, Benvolio; beat down their weapons.
Gentlemen, for shame forbear this outrage.
Tybalt, Mercutio, the prince expressly hath
Forbid this bandying in Verona streets.
Hold, Tybalt! good Mercutio!

> *'Tybalt under Romeo's arm thrusts Mercutio in*
> *and flies'*

Mercutio.   I am hurt.
A plague o' both your houses! I am sped.   90
Is he gone and hath nothing?
  Benvolio.   What, art thou hurt?
  Mercutio. Ay, ay, a scratch, a scratch; marry,
    'tis enough.
Where is my page? Go, villain, fetch a surgeon.

>   *[Page goes*

Romeo. Courage, man; the hurt cannot be much.
  Mercutio. No, 'tis not so deep as a well, nor so wide as
a church door, but 'tis enough, 'twill serve. Ask for me
tomorrow and you shall find me a grave man. I am
peppered, I warrant, for this world. A plague o' both
your houses! Zounds! A dog, a rat, a mouse, a cat, to
scratch a man to death! A braggart, a rogue, a villain, 100
that fights by the book of arithmetic! Why the devil
came you between us? I was hurt under your arm.
  Romeo. I thought all for the best.
  Mercutio. Help me into some house, Benvolio,
Or I shall faint. A plague o' both your houses!
They have made worms' meat of me. I have it,
And soundly too. Your houses!

>   *[Benvolio helps him away*

Romeo. This gentleman, the prince's near ally,
My very friend, hath got this mortal hurt
In my behalf, my reputation stained   110

With Tybalt's slander—Tybalt that an hour
Hath been my cousin. O sweet Juliet,
Thy beauty hath made me effeminate,
And in my temper softened valour's steel!

BENVOLIO returns

Benvolio. O Romeo, Romeo, brave Mercutio's
    dead.
That gallant spirit hath aspired the clouds,
Which too untimely here did scorn the earth.
    Romeo. This day's black fate on moe days
    doth depend;
This but begins the woe others must end.

TYBALT returns

120   *Benvolio.* Here comes the furious Tybalt
    back again.
    Romeo. Again! in triumph, and Mercutio slain!
Away to heaven, respective lenity,
And fire-eyed fury be my conduct now!
Now, Tybalt, take the 'villain' back again
That late thou gavest me, for Mercutio's soul
Is but a little way above our heads,
Staying for thine to keep him company.
Either thou or I, or both, must go with him.
    Tybalt. Thou wretched boy that didst consort
    him here
130 Shalt with him hence.
    Romeo.   This shall determine that.
                    ['*they fight, Tybalt falls*'
    Benvolio. Romeo, away, be gone!
The citizens are up, and Tybalt slain.
Stand not amazed. The prince will doom thee death
If thou art taken. Hence, be gone, away!

Romeo. O, I am Fortune's fool.
Benvolio.   Why dost thou stay?
                                              [*Romeo goes*

'*Enter Citizens*'

A Citizen. Which way ran he that killed Mercutio?
Tybalt, that murderer, which way ran he?
Benvolio. There lies that Tybalt.
A Citizen.   Up, sir, go with me:
I charge thee in the prince's name obey.

'*Enter* PRINCE, *old* MONTAGUE, CAPULET,
        their wives and all'

Prince. Where are the vile beginners of this fray?   140
Benvolio. O noble Prince, I can discover all
The unlucky manage of this fatal brawl.
There lies the man, slain by young Romeo,
That slew thy kinsman, brave Mercutio.
Lady Capulet. Tybalt, my cousin, O my
        brother's child!
O prince! O husband! O, the blood is spilled
Of my dear kinsman. Prince, as thou art true,
For blood of ours shed blood of Montague.
O cousin, cousin!
Prince. Benvolio, who began this bloody fray?   150
Benvolio. Tybalt, here slain, whom Romeo's hand
        did slay.
Romeo, that spoke him fair, bid him bethink
How nice the quarrel was, and urged withal
Your high displeasure. All this—utteréd
With gentle breath, calm look, knees humbly bowed—
Could not take truce with the unruly spleen
Of Tybalt deaf to peace, but that he tilts
With piercing steel at bold Mercutio's breast,

Who, all as hot, turns deadly point to point,
160 And, with a martial scorn, with one hand beats
Cold death aside and with the other sends
It back to Tybalt, whose dexterity
Retorts it. Romeo he cries aloud,
'Hold, friends! friends, part!' and, swifter than
    his tongue,
His agile arm beats down their fatal points,
And 'twixt them rushes; underneath whose arm
An envious thrust from Tybalt hit the life
Of stout Mercutio, and then Tybalt fled,
But by and by comes back to Romeo
170 Who had but newly entertained revenge,
And to 't they go like lightning; for, ere I
Could draw to part them, was stout Tybalt slain,
And, as he fell, did Romeo turn and fly:
This is the truth, or let Benvolio die.
   Lady Capulet. He is a kinsman to the Montague;
Affection makes him false, he speaks not true.
Some twenty of them fought in this black strife,
And all those twenty could but kill one life.
I beg for justice, which thou, Prince, must give:
180 Romeo slew Tybalt; Romeo must not live.
   Prince. Romeo slew him; he slew Mercutio.
Who now the price of his dear blood doth owe?
   Montague. Not Romeo, Prince; he was
    Mercutio's friend;
His fault concludes but what the law should end—
The life of Tybalt.
   Prince.   And for that offence
Immediately we do exile him hence.
I have an interest in your hearts' proceeding:
My blood for your rude brawls doth lie a-bleeding.
But I'll amerce you with so strong a fine

That you shall all repent the loss of mine.   190
I will be deaf to pleading and excuses;
Nor tears nor prayers shall purchase out abuses.
Therefore use none. Let Romeo hence in haste,
Else, when he is found, that hour is his last.
Bear hence this body, and attend our will.
Mercy but murders, pardoning those that kill.

                                                    [*they go*

[3. 2.]   *Capulet's house*

'*Enter* JULIET *alone*'

Juliet. Gallop apace, you fiery-footed steeds,
Towards Phoebus' lodging! Such a waggoner
As Phaëton would whip you to the west
And bring in cloudy night immediately.
Spread thy close curtain, love-performing night,
†That runaways' eyes may wink, and Romeo
Leap to these arms untalked of and unseen.
Lovers can see to do their amorous rites
By their own beauties; or, if love be blind,
It best agrees with night. Come, civil Night,   10
Thou sober-suited matron all in black,
And learn me how to lose a winning match,
Played for a pair of stainless maidenhoods.
Hood my unmanned blood, bating in my cheeks,
With thy black mantle till strange love, grown bold,
Think true love acted simple modesty.
Come, Night! Come, Romeo! Come, thou day
        in night;
For thou wilt lie upon the wings of night
Whiter than snow upon a raven's back.
Come, gentle Night; come, loving, black-
        browed Night: 20

Give me my Romeo; and, when he shall die,
Take him and cut him out in little stars,
And he will make the face of heaven so fine
That all the world will be in love with night
And pay no worship to the garish sun.
O, I have bought the mansion of a love,
But not possessed it; and though I am sold,
Not yet enjoyed. So tedious is this day
As is the night before some festival
30 To an impatient child that hath new robes
And may not wear them. O, here comes my nurse,

'Enter NURSE with cords'

And she brings news; and every tongue that speaks
But Romeo's name speaks heavenly eloquence.
Now, Nurse, what news? What hast thou there?
  The cords
That Romeo bid thee fetch?
 Nurse.   Ay, ay, the cords.
             [throws them down
 Juliet. Ay me, what news? Why dost thou wring
  thy hands?
 Nurse. Ah, weraday! He's dead, he's dead,
  he's dead!
We are undone, lady, we are undone.
Alack the day, he's gone, he's killed, he's dead!
40 *Juliet.* Can heaven be so envious?
 Nurse.   Romeo can,
Though heaven cannot. O Romeo, Romeo!
Who ever would have thought it? Romeo!
 Juliet. What devil art thou that dost torment
  me thus?
This torture should be roared in dismal hell.
Hath Romeo slain himself? Say thou but 'ay',

And that bare vowel 'I' shall poison more
Than the death-darting eye of cockatrice.
I am not I if there be such an 'I',
Or those eyes shut that makes thee answer 'ay'.
If he be slain, say 'ay', or, if not, 'no'.   50
Brief sounds determine of my weal or woe.

Nurse. I saw the wound, I saw it with mine eyes,
(God save the mark!) here on his manly breast.
A piteous corse, a bloody piteous corse,
Pale, pale as ashes, all bedaubed in blood,
All in gore blood; I swounded at the sight.

Juliet. O break, my heart! Poor bankrout, break
    at once!
To prison, eyes; ne'er look on liberty.
Vile earth, to earth resign, end motion here,
And thou and Romeo press one heavy bier!   60

Nurse. O Tybalt, Tybalt, the best friend I had!
O courteous Tybalt, honest gentleman,
That ever I should live to see thee dead!

Juliet. What storm is this that blows so contrary?
Is Romeo slaught'red? and is Tybalt dead?
My dearest cousin, and my dearer lord?
Then, dreadful trumpet, sound the general doom;
For who is living if those two are gone?

Nurse. Tybalt is gone and Romeo banishéd;
Romeo that killed him, he is banishéd.   70

Juliet. O God! did Romeo's hand shed
    Tybalt's blood?

Nurse. It did, it did! alas the day, it did!

Juliet. O serpent heart, hid with a flowering face!
Did ever dragon keep so fair a cave?
Beautiful tyrant, fiend angelical,
Dove-feathered raven, wolvish-ravening lamb!
Despiséd substance of divinest show,

Just opposite to what thou justly seemst—
A damnéd saint, an honourable villain!
80 O nature, what hadst thou to do in hell
When thou didst bower the spirit of a fiend
In mortal paradise of such sweet flesh?
Was ever book containing such vile matter
So fairly bound? O that deceit should dwell
In such a gorgeous palace!
 Nurse.   There's no trust,
No faith, no honesty in men; all perjured,
All forsworn, all naught, all dissemblers.
Ah, where's my man? Give me some aqua vitae.
These griefs, these woes, these sorrows make me old.
90 Shame come to Romeo!
 Juliet.   Blistered be thy tongue
For such a wish! He was not born to shame.
Upon his brow shame is ashamed to sit:
For 'tis a throne where honour may be crowned
Sole monarch of the universal earth.
O what a beast was I to chide at him!
 Nurse. Will you speak well of him that killed
  your cousin?
 Juliet. Shall I speak ill of him that is my husband?
Ah, poor my lord, what tongue shall smooth
  thy name
When I, thy three-hours wife, have mangled it?
100 But wherefore, villain, didst thou kill my cousin?
That villain cousin would have killed my husband.
Back, foolish tears, back to your native spring!
Your tributary drops belong to woe
Which you, mistaking, offer up to joy.
My husband lives, that Tybalt would have slain,
And Tybalt's dead that would have slain my husband:
All this is comfort; wherefore weep I then?

Some word there was, worser than Tybalt's death,
That murd'red me. I would forget it fain,
But oh, it presses to my memory   110
Like damnéd guilty deeds to sinners' minds—
'Tybalt is dead and Romeo banishéd'.
That 'banishéd', that one word 'banishéd',
Hath slain ten thousand Tybalts. Tybalt's death
Was woe enough if it had ended there:
Or, if sour woe delights in fellowship
And needly will be ranked with other griefs,
Why followed not, when she said 'Tybalt's dead',
'Thy father', or 'thy mother', nay, or both,
Which modern lamentation might have moved?   120
But, with a rearward following Tybalt's death,
'Romeo is banishéd'! To speak that word
Is father, mother, Tybalt, Romeo, Juliet,
All slain, all dead: 'Romeo is banishéd'!
There is no end, no limit, measure, bound,
In that word's death; no words can that
        woe sound.
Where is my father and my mother, Nurse?
  Nurse. Weeping and wailing over Tybalt's corse.
Will you go to them? I will bring you thither.
  Juliet. Wash they his wounds with tears? Mine
        shall be spent,   130
When theirs are dry, for Romeo's banishment.
Take up those cords. Poor ropes, you are beguiled,
Both you and I, for Romeo is exiled.
He made you for a highway to my bed,
But I, a maid, die maiden-widowéd.
Come, cords; come, Nurse: I'll to my wedding bed,
And death, not Romeo, take my maidenhead!
  Nurse. Hie to your chamber. I'll find Romeo
To comfort you: I wot well where he is.

140 Hark ye, your Romeo will be here at night:
I'll to him; he is hid at Lawrence' cell.
    Juliet. O find him! Give this ring to my true knight
And bid him come to take his last farewell.

                                                    [*they go*

[3. 3.]   *Friar Lawrence's cell with his
               study at the back*

                Enter FRIAR

  Friar. Romeo, come forth; come forth, thou
      fearful man.
Affliction is enamoured of thy parts,
And thou art wedded to calamity.

            Enter ROMEO *from the study*

  Romeo. Father, what news? What is the
      prince's doom?
What sorrow craves acquaintance at my hand
That I yet know not?
    Friar.   Too familiar
Is my dear son with such sour company!
I bring thee tidings of the prince's doom.
  Romeo. What less than doomsday is the
      prince's doom?
10 *Friar.* A gentler judgment vanished from his lips;
Not body's death, but body's banishment.
  Romeo. Ha, banishment? Be merciful, say 'death':
For exile hath more terror in his look,
Much more than death: do not say 'banishment'.
  Friar. Hence from Verona art thou banishéd.
Be patient, for the world is broad and wide.
  Romeo. There is no world without Verona walls,
But purgatory, torture, hell itself:

Hence banishéd is banished from the world,
And world's exile is death. Then 'banishéd'   20
Is death mis-termed. Calling death 'banishéd',
Thou cut'st my head off with a golden axe,
And smilest upon the stroke that murders me.

Friar. O deadly sin! O rude unthankfulness!
Thy fault our law calls death, but the kind Prince,
Taking thy part, hath rushed aside the law,
And turned that black word 'death' to 'banishment'.
This is dear mercy, and thou seest it not.

Romeo. 'Tis torture and not mercy. Heaven is here
Where Juliet lives, and every cat and dog   30
And little mouse, every unworthy thing,
Live here in heaven and may look on her,
But Romeo may not. More validity,
More honourable state, more courtship, lives
In carrion flies than Romeo: they may seize
On the white wonder of dear Juliet's hand,
And steal immortal blessing from her lips,
Who even in pure and vestal modesty
Still blush, as thinking their own kisses sin;
This may flies do, when I from this must fly;   40
And say'st thou yet that exile is not death?
But Romeo may not—he is banishéd.
Flies may do this, but I from this must fly:
They are free men, but I am banishéd.
Hadst thou no poison mixed, no sharp-ground knife,
No sudden mean of death, though ne'er so mean,
But 'banishéd' to kill me? 'Banishéd'!
O friar, the damnéd use that word in hell:
Howling attends it. How hast thou the heart,
Being a divine, a ghostly confessor,   50
A sin-absolver, and my friend professed,
To mangle me with that word 'banishéd'?

Friar. Thou fond mad man, hear me a little speak.

Romeo. O thou wilt speak again of banishment.

Friar. I'll give thee armour to keep off that word—
Adversity's sweet milk, philosophy,
To comfort thee though thou art banishéd.

Romeo. Yet 'banishéd'? Hang up philosophy!
Unless philosophy can make a Juliet,

60 Displant a town, reverse a prince's doom,
It helps not, it prevails not; talk no more.

Friar. O then I see that madmen have no ears.

Romeo. How should they, when that wise men have
no eyes?

Friar. Let me dispute with thee of thy estate.

Romeo. Thou canst not speak of that thou dost
not feel.
Wert thou as young as I, Juliet thy love,
An hour but married, Tybalt murderéd,
Doting like me, and like me banishéd,
Then mightst thou speak, then mightst thou tear
thy hair,

70 And fall upon the ground as I do now,
Taking the measure of an unmade grave.

[knocking without

Friar. Arise; one knocks. Good Romeo, hide thyself.

Romeo. Not I, unless the breath of heartsick groans
Mist-like infold me from the search of eyes.

[knocking again

Friar. Hark, how they knock!—Who's there?—
Romeo, arise;
Thou wilt be taken.—Stay awhile!—Stand up;

[louder knocking

Run to my study.—By and by!—God's will,
What simpleness is this?—I come, I come?

[knocking yet again

Who knocks so hard? Whence come you? What's
    your will?
  Nurse. [*from without*] Let me come in and you shall
    know my errand: 80
I come from Lady Juliet.
  Friar.   Welcome then.

           '*Enter* NURSE'

  Nurse. O holy friar, O tell me, holy friar,
Where is my lady's lord? Where's Romeo?
  Friar. There on the ground, with his own tears
    made drunk.
  Nurse. O he is even in my mistress' case,
Just in her case.
  Friar.   O woeful sympathy:
Piteous predicament!
  Nurse.   Even so lies she,
Blubbering and weeping, weeping and blubbering.
Stand up, stand up! Stand an you be a man;
For Juliet's sake, for her sake rise and stand: 90
Why should you fall into so deep an O?
  Romeo. [*rising*] Nurse!
  Nurse.   Ah sir, ah sir, death's the end of all.
  Romeo. Spakest thou of Juliet? How is it with her?
Doth not she think me an old murderer,
Now I have stained the childhood of our joy
With blood removed but little from her own?
Where is she? and how doth she? and what says
My concealed lady to our cancelled love?
  Nurse. O she says nothing, sir, but weeps and weeps,
And now falls on her bed, and then starts up,   100
And Tybalt calls, and then on Romeo cries,
And then down falls again.
  Romeo.   As if that name,

Shot from the deadly level of a gun,
Did murder her, as that name's cursèd hand
Murdered·her kinsman. O tell me, friar, tell me,
In what vile part of this anatomy
Doth my name lodge? Tell me, that I may sack
The hateful mansion.   ['*he offers to stab himself, and*
                            Nurse snatches the dagger away'
Friar.   Hold thy desperate hand!
Art thou a man? Thy form cries out thou art:
110 Thy tears are womanish, thy wild acts denote
The unreasonable fury of a beast.
Unseemly woman in a seeming man,
And ill-beseeming beast in seeming both!
Thou hast amazed me. By my holy order,
I thought thy disposition better tempered.
Hast thou slain Tybalt? Wilt thou slay thyself?
And slay thy lady, that in thy life lives,
By doing damnèd hate upon thyself?
Why rail'st thou on thy birth, the heaven, and earth,
120 Since birth, and heaven, and earth, all three do meet
In thee at once, which thou at once wouldst lose?
Fie, fie! thou sham'st thy shape, thy love, thy wit,
Which like a usurer abound'st in all,
And usest none in that true use indeed
Which should bedeck thy shape, thy love, thy wit.
Thy noble shape is but a form of wax,
Digressing from the valour of a man;
Thy dear love sworn but hollow perjury,
Killing that love which thou hast vowed to cherish;
130 Thy wit, that ornament to shape and love,
Misshapen in the conduct of them both,
Like powder in a skilless soldier's flask
Is set afire by thine own ignorance,
And thou dismembered with thine own defence.

What, rouse thee, man! Thy Juliet is alive,
For whose dear sake thou wast but lately dead.
There art thou happy. Tybalt would kill thee,
But thou slewest Tybalt. There art thou happy.
The law that threatened death becomes thy friend,
And turns it to exile. There art thou happy too.   140
A pack of blessings light upon thy back;
Happiness courts thee in her best array;
But, like a misbehaved and sullen wench,
Thou pouts upon thy fortune and thy love.
Take heed, take heed, for such die miserable.
Go get thee to thy love, as was decreed;
Ascend her chamber; hence and comfort her.
But look thou stay not till the watch be set,
For then thou canst not pass to Mantua,
Where thou shalt live till we can find a time   150
To blaze your marriage, reconcile your friends,
Beg pardon of the prince, and call thee back
With twenty hundred thousand times more joy
Than thou wentst forth in lamentation.
Go before, Nurse. Commend me to thy lady,
And bid her hasten all the house to bed,
Which heavy sorrow makes them apt unto.
Romeo is coming.
  Nurse. O Lord, I could have stayed here all
        the night
To hear good counsel; O what learning is!   160
My lord, I'll tell my lady you will come.
  Romeo. Do so, and bid my sweet prepare to chide.

        '*Nurse offers to go in and turns again*'

  Nurse. Here, sir, a ring she bid me give you, sir.
Hie you, make haste, for it grows very late.   [*she goes*
  Romeo. How well my comfort is revived by this.

Friar. Go hence; goodnight; and here stands all
    your state:
Either be gone before the watch be set,
Or by the break of day disguised from hence.
Sojourn in Mantua. I'll find out your man,
170 And he shall signify from time to time
Every good hap to you that chances here.
Give me thy hand. 'Tis late; farewell, goodnight.
   Romeo. But that a joy past joy calls out on me,
It were a grief so brief to part with thee.
Farewell.   [*they go*

[3. 4.]   *Capulet's house*

'*Enter old* CAPULET, *his wife, and* PARIS'

   Capulet. Things have fall'n out, sir, so unluckily
That we have had no time to move our daughter.
Look you, she loved her kinsman Tybalt dearly,
And so did I. Well, we were born to die.
'Tis very late; she'll not come down tonight.
I promise you, but for your company,
I would have been abed an hour ago.
   Paris. These times of woe afford no times
    to woo.
Madam, goodnight; commend me to your daughter.
10   *Lady Capulet.* I will, and know her mind
    early tomorrow;
Tonight she's mewed up to her heaviness.

Paris offers to go; Capulet calls him again

   Capulet. Sir Paris, I will make a desperate tender
Of my child's love: I think she will be ruled
In all respects by me: nay more, I doubt it not.
Wife, go you to her ere you go to bed;

Acquaint her ear of my son Paris' love,
And bid her, mark you me, on Wednesday next—
But soft, what day is this?
  Paris.   Monday, my lord.
  Capulet. Monday, ha, ha; well, Wednesday is
      too soon;
O' Thursday let it be— O' Thursday, tell her,   20
She shall be married to this noble earl—
Will you be ready? Do you like this haste?
We'll keep no great ado; a friend or two:
For hark you, Tybalt being slain so late,
It may be thought we held him carelessly,
Being our kinsman, if we revel much:
Therefore we'll have some half a dozen friends,
And there an end. But what say you to Thursday?
  Paris. My lord, I would that Thursday
      were tomorrow.
  Capulet. Well, get you gone. O' Thursday be
     it then.   30
Go you to Juliet ere you go to bed;
Prepare her, wife, against this wedding day.
Farewell, my lord. Light to my chamber, ho!
Afore me, 'tis so very late, that we
May call it early by and by. Goodnight.   [*they go*

[3. 5.]   *Juliet's bedroom: to one side the*
         window above the Orchard; to the other a door

      ROMEO and JULIET stand by the window

Juliet. Wilt thou be gone? It is not yet near day.
It was the nightingale, and not the lark,
That pierced the fearful hollow of thine ear.
Nightly she sings on yond pomegranate tree.

Believe me, love, it was the nightingale.

Romeo. It was the lark, the herald of the morn;
No nightingale. Look, love, what envious streaks
Do lace the severing clouds in yonder east.
Night's candles are burnt out, and jocund day
10 Stands tiptoe on the misty mountain tops.
I must be gone and live, or stay and die.

Juliet. Yond light is not daylight; I know it, I:
It is some meteor that the sun exhaled
To be to thee this night a torchbearer
And light thee on thy way to Mantua.
Therefore stay yet; thou needst not to be gone.

Romeo. Let me be ta'en, let me be put
        to death;
I am content, so thou wilt have it so.
I'll say yon gray is not the morning's eye,
20 'Tis but the pale reflex of Cynthia's brow;
Nor that is not the lark whose notes do beat
The vaulty heaven so high above our heads.
I have more care to stay than will to go:
Come, death, and welcome! Juliet wills it so.
How is't, my soul? Let's talk; it is not day.

Juliet. It is, it is! Hie hence, be gone, away!
It is the lark that sings so out of tune,
Straining harsh discords and unpleasing sharps.
Some say the lark makes sweet division:
30 This doth not so, for she divideth us.
Some say the lark and loathéd toad changed eyes;
O now I would they had changed voices too,
Since arm from arm that voice doth us affray,
Hunting thee hence with hunt's-up to the day.
O now be gone! More light and light it grows.

Romeo. More light and light, more dark and dark
    our woes.

'*Enter* NURSE *hastily*'

Nurse. Madam!

Juliet. Nurse?

Nurse. Your lady mother is coming to your chamber.
The day is broke; be wary, look about.   40
                    [*she goes; Juliet bolts the door*

Juliet. Then, window, let day in and let life out.

Romeo. Farewell, farewell; one kiss, and I'll descend.
                    [*he lowers the ladder and descends*

Juliet. Art thou gone so, love, lord, ay
        husband, friend?
I must hear from thee every day in the hour,
For in a minute there are many days.
O, by this count I shall be much in years
Ere I again behold my Romeo.

Romeo. [*from the orchard*] Farewell!
I will omit no opportunity
That may convey my greetings, love, to thee.   50

Juliet. O, think'st thou we shall ever meet again?

Romeo. I doubt it not; and all these woes shall serve
For sweet discourses in our times to come.

Juliet. O God, I have an ill-divining soul!
Methinks I see thee, now thou art so low,
As one dead in the bottom of a tomb.
Either my eyesight fails or thou look'st pale.

Romeo. And trust me, love, in my eye so do you.
Dry sorrow drinks our blood. Adieu, adieu!
                                        [*he goes*

Juliet. O Fortune, Fortune, all men call thee fickle;   60
If thou art fickle, what dost thou with him
That is renowned for faith? Be fickle, Fortune:
For then I hope thou wilt not keep him long,
But send him back.

Lady Capulet. [*without the door*] Ho, daughter, are
   you up?
Juliet. [*pulls up and conceals the ladder*]
Who is't that calls? It is my lady mother.
Is she not down so late, or up so early?
What unaccustomed cause procures her hither?
                                    [*she unlocks the door*

Enter LADY CAPULET

Lady Capulet. Why, how now, Juliet?
Juliet.   Madam, I am not well.
Lady Capulet. Evermore weeping for your
   cousin's death?
70 What, wilt thou wash him from his grave with tears?
An if thou couldst, thou couldst not make him live:
Therefore have done—some grief shows much
         of love,
But much of grief shows still some want of wit.
   Juliet. Yet let me weep for such a feeling loss.
   Lady Capulet. So shall you feel the loss, but not
      the friend
Which you weep for.
   Juliet.   Feeling so the loss,
I cannot choose but ever weep the friend.
   Lady Capulet. Well, girl, thou weep'st not so much
      for his death,
As that the villain lives which slaughtered him.
80   *Juliet.* What villain, madam?
   Lady Capulet.   That same villain Romeo.
   (*Juliet.* Villain and he be many miles asunder.
[*aloud*] God pardon him; I do, with all my heart:
And yet no man like he doth grieve my heart.
   Lady Capulet. That is because the traitor
      murderer lives.

Juliet. Ay, madam, from the reach of these
    my hands.
Would none but I might venge my cousin's death!
Lady Capulet. We will have vengeance for it, fear
    thou not.
Then weep no more. ''ll send to one in Mantua,
Where that same banished runagate doth live,
Shall give him such an unaccustomed dram   90
That he shall soon keep Tybalt company;
And then I hope thou wilt be satisfied.
Juliet. Indeed I never shall be satisfied
With Romeo till I behold him—dead—
Is my poor heart so for a kinsman vexed.
Madam, if you could find out but a man
To bear a poison, I would temper it
That Romeo should upon receipt thereof
Soon sleep in quiet. O how my heart abhors
To hear him named and cannot come to him   100
To wreak the love I bore my cousin
Upon his body that hath slaughtered him.
Lady Capulet. Find thou the means and I'll find such
    a man.
But now I'll tell thee joyful tidings, girl.
Juliet. And joy comes well in such a
    needy time.
What are they, I beseech your ladyship?
Lady Capulet. Well, well, thou hast a careful
    father, child;
One who, to put thee from thy heaviness,
Hath sorted out a sudden day of joy
That thou expects not, nor I looked not for.   110
Juliet. Madam, in happy time! What day is that?
Lady Capulet. Marry, my child, early next
    Thursday morn

The gallant, young, and noble gentleman,
The County Paris, at Saint Peter's Church
Shall happily make thee there a joyful bride.
   Juliet. Now by Saint Peter's Church, and
      Peter too,
He shall not make me there a joyful bride.
I wonder at this haste, that I must wed
Ere he that should be husband comes to woo.
120 I pray you tell my lord and father, madam,
I will not marry yet; and when I do, I swear
It shall be Romeo, whom you know I hate,
Rather than Paris. These are news indeed!
   Lady Capulet. Here comes your father; tell him
      so yourself,
And see how he will take it at your hands.

'Enter CAPULET and NURSE'

   Capulet. When the sun sets, the air doth
      drizzle dew;
But for the sunset of my brother's son
It rains downright.
How now, a conduit, girl? What, still in tears?
130 Evermore showering? In one little body
Thou counterfeits a bark, a sea, a wind:
For still thy eyes, which I may call the sea,
Do ebb and flow with tears; the bark thy body is,
Sailing in this salt flood; the winds thy sighs,
Who raging with thy tears, and they with them,
Without a sudden calm will overset
Thy tempest-tosséd body. How now, wife?
Have you delivered to her our decree?
   Lady Capulet. Ay, sir; but she will none, she gives
      you thanks.
140 I would the fool were married to her grave!

Capulet. Soft, take me with you, take me with
    you, wife.
How? Will she none? Doth she not give us thanks?
Is she not proud? Doth she not count her blest,
Unworthy as she is, that we have wrought
So worthy a gentleman to be her bride?
    Juliet. Not proud you have, but thankful that
    you have.
Proud can I never be of what I hate,
But thankful even for hate that is meant love.
    Capulet. How how! how how, chop-logic! what
    is this?
'Proud', and 'I thank you', and 'I thank you not',   150
And yet 'not proud', mistress minion you?
Thank me no thankings nor proud me no prouds,
But fettle your fine joints 'gainst Thursday next
To go with Paris to Saint Peter's Church,
Or I will drag thee on a hurdle thither.
Out, you green-sickness carrion! out, you baggage!
You tallow-face!
    Lady Capulet.   Fie, fie! what, are you mad?
    Juliet. [*kneeling*] Good father, I beseech you on
    my knees,
Hear me with patience but to speak a word.
    Capulet. Hang thee, young baggage!
    disobedient wretch!   160
I tell thee what; get thee to church o' Thursday,
Or never after look me in the face.
Speak not, reply not, do not answer me!
My fingers itch. Wife, we scarce thought us blest
That God had lent us but this only child;
But now I see this one is one too much,
And that we have a curse in having her.
Out on her, hilding!

Nurse.   God in heaven bless her!
You are to blame, my lord, to rate her so.

170 *Capulet.* And why, my Lady Wisdom? Hold
      your tongue,
Good Prudence. Smatter with your gossips, go!
  Nurse. I speak no treason.
  Capulet.   O Godigoden!
  Nurse. May not one speak?
  Capulet.   Peace, you mumbling fool!
Utter your gravity o'er a gossip's bowl,
For here we need it not.
  Lady Capulet.   You are too hot.
  Capulet. God's bread! it makes me mad. Day, night,
      work, play,
Alone, in company, still my care hath been
To have her matched; and having now provided
A gentleman of noble parentage,

180 Of fair demesnes, youthful and nobly trained,
Stuffed, as they say, with honourable parts,
Proportioned as one's thought would wish a man—
And then to have a wretched puling fool,
A whining mammet, in her fortune's tender,
To answer 'I'll not wed, I cannot love;
I am too young, I pray you pardon me'.
But, an you will not wed, I'll pardon you—
Graze where you will; you shall not house with me.
Look to't, think on't; I do not use to jest.

190 Thursday is near. Lay hand on heart; advise.
An you be mine, I'll give you to my friend;
An you be not, hang, beg, starve, die in the streets,
For by my soul I'll ne'er acknowledge thee,
Nor what is mine shall never do thee good:
Trust to 't; bethink you; I'll not be forsworn.

                        [he goes

Juliet. Is there no pity sitting in the clouds
That sees into the bottom of my grief?
O sweet my mother, cast me not away!
Delay this marriage for a month, a week;
Or, if you do not, make the bridal bed   200
In that dim monument where Tybalt lies.
   Lady Capulet. Talk not to me, for I'll not speak
     a word;
Do as thou wilt, for I have done with thee.

                                 [*she goes*

   Juliet. O God!—O nurse, how shall this
     be prevented?
My husband is on earth, my faith in heaven;
How shall that faith return again to earth,
Unless that husband send it me from heaven
By leaving earth? Comfort me, counsel me.
Alack, alack, that heaven should practise stratagems
Upon so soft a subject as myself!   210
What sayst thou? Hast thou not a word of joy?
Some comfort, nurse.
   Nurse.   Faith, here it is. Romeo
Is banishéd; and all the world to nothing
That he dares ne'er come back to challenge you;
Or, if he do, it needs must be by stealth.
Then, since the case so stands as now it doth,
I think it best you married with the County.
O, he's a lovely gentleman!
Romeo's a dishclout to him. An eagle, madam,
Hath not so green, so quick, so fair an eye   220
As Paris hath. Beshrew my very heart,
I think you are happy in this second match,
For it excels your first; or, if it did not,
Your first is dead—or 'twere as good he were
As living here and you no use of him.

                                   6-2

Juliet. Speakst thou from thy heart?

Nurse. And from my soul too; else beshrew
   them both.

Juliet. Amen!

Nurse. What?

230 *Juliet.* Well, thou hast comforted me
         marvellous much.

Go in and tell my lady I am gone,

Having displeased my father, to Lawrence' cell

To make confession and to be absolved.

Nurse. Marry, I will; and this is wisely done.

                              [*she goes*

Juliet. Ancient damnation! O most wicked fiend!

Is it more sin to wish me thus forsworn,

Or to dispraise my lord with that same tongue

Which she hath praised him with above compare

So many thousand times? Go, counsellor!

240 Thou and my bosom henceforth shall be twain.

I'll to the friar to know his remedy.

If all else fail, myself have power to die.   [*she goes*

[4. 1.]   *Friar Lawrence's cell*

         '*Enter* FRIAR *and County* PARIS'

Friar. On Thursday, sir? The time is very short.

Paris. My father Capulet will have it so,

And I am nothing slow to slack his haste.

Friar. You say you do not know the lady's mind?

Uneven is the course; I like it not.

Paris. Immoderately she weeps for Tybalt's death,

And therefore have I little talked of love,

For Venus smiles not in a house of tears.

Now, sir, her father counts it dangerous

That she do give her sorrow so much sway,   10
And in his wisdom hastes our marriage
To stop the inundation of her tears,
Which, too much minded by herself alone,
May be put from her by society.
Now do you know the reason of this haste.
  (*Friar*. I would I knew not why it should
          be slowed—
Look, sir, here comes the lady toward my cell.

'Enter JULIET'

Paris. Happily met, my lady and my wife!
Juliet. That may be, sir, when I may be a wife.
Paris. That 'may be' must be, love, on
          Thursday next.   20
Juliet. What must be shall be.
Friar.   That's a certain text.
Paris. Come you to make confession to this father?
Juliet. To answer that, I should confess to you.
Paris. Do not deny to him that you love me.
Juliet. I will confess to you that I love him.
Paris. So will ye, I am sure, that you love me.
Juliet. If I do so, it will be of more price,
Being spoke behind your back, than to your face.
Paris. Poor soul, thy face is much abused with tears.
Juliet. The tears have got small victory by that,   3c
For it was bad enough before their spite.
Paris. Thou wrong'st it more than tears with
          that report.
Juliet. That is no slander, sir, which is a truth;
And what I spake, I spake it to my face.
Paris. Thy face is mine, and thou hast sland'red it.
Juliet. It may be so, for it is not mine own.—
Are you at leisure, holy father, now,

Or shall I come to you at evening mass?

Friar. My leisure serves me, pensive daughter, now.
40 My lord, we must entreat the time alone.

Paris. God shield I should disturb devotion!
Juliet, on Thursday early will I rouse ye;
Till then adieu, and keep this holy kiss.

> [*kisses her, and departs*

Juliet. O shut the door, and, when thou hast
    done so,
Come weep with me—past hope, past cure, past help.

Friar. O Juliet, I already know thy grief;
It strains me past the compass of my wits.
I hear thou must, and nothing may prorogue it,
On Thursday next be married to this County.

50 *Juliet.* Tell me not, friar, that thou hearest of this,
Unless thou tell me how I may prevent it.
If in thy wisdom thou canst give no help,
Do thou but call my resolution wise
And with this knife I'll help it presently.
God joined my heart and Romeo's, thou our hands;
And ere this hand, by thee to Romeo's sealed,
Shall be the label to another deed,
Or my true heart with treacherous revolt
Turn to another, this shall slay them both:
60 Therefore, out of thy long-experienced time,
Give me some present counsel; or, behold,
'Twixt my extremes and me this bloody knife
Shall play the umpire, arbitrating that
Which the commission of thy years and art
Could to no issue of true honour bring.
Be not so long to speak: I long to die
If what thou speak'st speak not of remedy.

Friar. Hold, daughter. I do spy a kind of hope,
Which craves as desperate an execution

As that is desperate which we would prevent.
If, rather than to marry County Paris,
Thou hast the strength of will to slay thyself,
Then is it likely thou wilt undertake
A thing like death to chide away this shame,
That copest with death himself to scape from it;
And, if thou darest, I'll give thee remedy.

Juliet. O bid me leap, rather than marry Paris,
From off the battlements of any tower,
Or walk in thievish ways, or bid me lurk
Where serpents are; chain me with roaring bears,   80
Or hide me nightly in a charnel house,
O'ercovered quite with dead men's rattling bones,
With reeky shanks and yellow chapless skulls;
Or bid me go into a new-made grave
And lay me with a dead man in his shroud—
Things that, to hear them told, have made
     me tremble—
And I will do it without fear or doubt,
To live an unstained wife to my sweet love.

Friar. Hold, then. Go home, be merry,
     give consent
To marry Paris. Wednesday is tomorrow.   90
Tomorrow night look that thou lie alone;
Let not the nurse lie with thee in thy chamber.
Take thou this vial, being then in bed,
And this distilléd liquor drink thou off,
When presently through all thy veins shall run
A cold and drowsy humour, for no pulse
Shall keep his native progress, but surcease;
No warmth, no breath, shall testify thou livest;
The roses in thy lips and cheeks shall fade
To wanny ashes, thy eyes' windows fall   100
Like death when he shuts up the day of life.

Each part, deprived of supple government,
Shall stiff and stark and cold appear like death;
And in this borrowed likeness of shrunk death
Thou shalt continue two and forty hours,
And then awake as from a pleasant sleep.
Now, when the bridegroom in the morning comes
To rouse thee from thy bed, there art thou dead.
Then, as the manner of our country is,
110 In thy best robes, uncovered on the bier,
Thou shalt be borne to that same ancient vault
Where all the kindred of the Capulets lie.
In the meantime, against thou shalt awake,
Shall Romeo by my letters know our drift,
And hither shall he come; and he and I
Will watch thy waking, and that very night
Shall Romeo bear thee hence to Mantua.
And this shall free thee from this present shame,
If no inconstant toy nor womanish fear
120 Abate thy valour in the acting it.
 Juliet. Give me, give me! O tell not me of fear!
 Friar. Hold, get you gone! Be strong
  and prosperous
In this resolve. I'll send a friar with speed
To Mantua with my letters to thy lord.
 Juliet. Love give me strength! and strength shall
  help afford.
Farewell, dear father.   *[they go*

[4. 2.]   *Capulet's house*

*Enter CAPULET, LADY CAPULET, NURSE
and two or three Servingmen*

Capulet [*giving a paper*]. So many guests invite as here
  are writ.   [*servingman goes out with it*
[*to another*] Sirrah, go hire me twenty cunning cooks.
Servingman. You shall have none ill, sir; for I'll try
if they can lick their fingers.
Capulet. How canst thou try them so?
Servingman. Marry, sir, 'tis an ill cook that cannot
lick his own fingers: therefore he that cannot lick his
fingers goes not with me.
Capulet. Go, be gone.   [*he goes*
We shall be much unfurnished for this time.   10
What, is my daughter gone to Friar Lawrence?
Nurse. Ay, forsooth.
Capulet. Well, he may chance to do some good
  on her.
A peevish self-willed harlotry it is.

'*Enter JULIET*'

Nurse. See where she comes from shrift with
  merry look.
Capulet. How now, my headstrong? Where have you
  been gadding?
Juliet. Where I have learned me to repent the sin
Of disobedient opposition
To you and your behests, and am enjoined
By holy Lawrence to fall prostrate here   20
To beg your pardon. [*abasing herself*] Pardon,
  I beseech you!
Henceforward I am ever ruled by you.

Capulet. Send for the County: go tell him of this.
I'll have this knot knit up tomorrow morning.

Juliet. I met the youthful lord at Lawrence' cell
And gave him what becoméd love I might,
Not stepping o'er the bounds of modesty.

Capulet. Why, I am glad on't; this is well.
    Stand up.
This is as 't should be. Let me see, the County:
30 Ay, marry, go, I say, and fetch him hither.
Now, afore God, this reverend holy friar,
All our whole city is much bound to him.

Juliet. Nurse, will you go with me into my closet
To help me sort such needful ornaments
As you think fit to furnish me tomorrow?

Lady Capulet. No, not till Thursday; there is
    time enough.

Capulet. Go, nurse, go with her; we'll to
    church tomorrow.   [*Nurse departs with Juliet*

Lady Capulet. We shall be short in our provision;
'Tis now near night.

Capulet.   Tush, I will stir about,
40 And all things shall be well, I warrant thee, wife.
Go thou to Juliet; help to deck up her.
I'll not to bed tonight. Let me alone;
I'll play the housewife for this once. What, ho!
They are all forth; well, I will walk myself
To County Paris, to prepare up him
Against tomorrow. My heart is wondrous light
Since this same wayward girl is so reclaimed. [*they go*

[4. 3.]   *Juliet's chamber; at the back a bed*
with curtains

'*Enter* JULIET *and* NURSE'

Juliet. Ay, those attires are best. But,
  gentle nurse,
I pray thee leave me to myself tonight:
For I have need of many orisons
To move the heavens to smile upon my state,
Which well thou knowest is cross and full of sin.

Enter LADY CAPULET

Lady Capulet. What, are you busy, ho? Need you
  my help?
Juliet. No, madam, we have culled such necessaries
As are behoveful for our state tomorrow.
So please you, let me now be left alone,
And let the nurse this night sit up with you,   10
For I am sure you have your hands full all
In this so sudden business.
Lady Capulet.   Good night.
Get thee to bed and rest, for thou hast need.
                              [*she departs with the Nurse*
Juliet. Farewell! God knows when we shall
  meet again.
I have a faint cold fear thrills through my veins
That almost freezes up the heat of life.
I'll call them back again to comfort me.
Nurse!—What should she do here?
My dismal scene I needs must act alone.
Come, vial!   20
What if this mixture do not work at all?
Shall I be married then tomorrow morning?

No, no! This shall forbid it. Lie thou there.

[laying down her knife

What if it be a poison which the friar
Subtly hath minist'red to have me dead,
Lest in this marriage he should be dishonoured
Because he married me before to Romeo?
I fear it is; and yet methinks it should not,
For he hath still been tried a holy man.
30 How if, when I am laid into the tomb,
I wake before the time that Romeo
Come to redeem me? There's a fearful point!
Shall I not then be stifled in the vault,
To whose foul mouth no healthsome air breathes in,
And there die strangled ere my Romeo comes?
Or, if I live, is it not very like
The horrible conceit of death and night,
Together with the terror of the place—
As in a vault, an ancient receptacle
40 Where for this many hundred years the bones
Of all my buried ancestors are packed;
Where bloody Tybalt, yet but green in earth,
Lies festering in his shroud; where, as they say,
At some hours in the night spirits resort—
Alack, alack, is it not like that I,
So early waking—what with loathsome smells,
And shrieks like mandrakes' torn out of
the earth,
That living mortals, hearing them, run mad—
O, if I wake, shall I not be distraught,
50 Environéd with all these hideous fears,
And madly play with my forefathers' joints,
And pluck the mangled Tybalt from his shroud,
And, in this rage, with some great kinsman's bone,
As with a club, dash out my desp'rate brains?

O, look! Methinks I see my cousin's ghost
Seeking out Romeo, that did spit his body
Upon a rapier's point. Stay, Tybalt, stay!
Romeo, I come! this do I drink to thee.

> ['*she falls upon her bed within
> the curtains*'

[4. 4.]   *Hall in Capulet's house*

Enter LADY CAPULET *and* 'NURSE,
with herbs'

Lady Capulet. Hold, take these keys and fetch more
    spices, nurse.
Nurse. They call for dates and quinces in the pastry.

'*Enter old* CAPULET'

Capulet. Come, stir, stir, stir! The second cock
    hath crowed:
The curfew bell hath rung, 'tis three o'clock.
Look to the baked meats, good Angelica;
Spare not for cost.
Nurse.   Go, you cot-quean, go,
Get you to bed. Faith, you'll be sick tomorrow
For this night's watching.
Capulet. No, not a whit. What, I have watched
    ere now
All night for lesser cause, and ne'er been sick.   10
Lady Capulet. Ay, you have been a mouse-hunt in
    your time,
But I will watch you from such watching now.

> [*she hurries out with Nurse*
Capulet. A jealous hood, a jealous hood!

*'Enter three or four with spits and
logs and baskets'*

                                    Now, fellow, what is there?
First Servingman. Things for the cook, sir; but I
    know not what.
Capulet. Make haste, make haste. [1 *servingman goes*]
                                    Sirrah, fetch drier logs.
Call Peter; he will show thee where they are.
Second Servingman. I have a head, sir, that will find
    out logs
And never trouble Peter for the matter.
Capulet. Mass, and well said; a merry whoreson, ha!
20 Thou shalt be loggerhead.   [2 *servingman goes*]
    Good faith, 'tis day!
The County will be here with music straight,
For so he said he would. [*music*] I hear him near.
Nurse! Wife! What, ho! What, nurse, I say!

'Enter Nurse*'*

Go waken Juliet; go and trim her up.
I'll go and chat with Paris. Hie, make haste,
Make haste! The bridegroom he is come already:
Make haste, I say.   [*they go*

[4. 5.]   *Juliet's chamber; the curtains
            closed about the bed*

                Enter Nurse

Nurse. Mistress! what, mistress! Juliet! Fast, I warrant
    her, she.
Why, lamb! why, lady! Fie, you slug-a-bed!
Why, love, I say! madam! sweetheart! why, bride!

What, not a word? You take your pennyworths now!
Sleep for a week; for the next night, I warrant,
The County Paris hath set up his rest
That you shall rest but little. God forgive me!
Marry, and amen! How sound is she asleep!
I needs must wake her. Madam, madam, madam!
Ay, let the County take you in your bed,   10
He'll fright you up, i'faith! Will it not be?

         [draws back the curtains

What, dressed, and in your clothes, and down again?
I must needs wake you. Lady, lady, lady! *[shakes her*
Alas, alas! Help, help! My lady's dead!
O weraday that ever I was born!
Some aqua-vitae, ho! My lord! my lady!

     Enter LADY CAPULET

Lady Capulet. What noise is here?
Nurse.   O lamentable day!
Lady Capulet. What is the matter?
Nurse.   Look, look! O heavy day!
Lady Capulet. O me, O me! My child, my only life!
Revive, look up, or I will die with thee!   20
Help, help! Call help.

      Enter CAPULET

Capulet. For shame, bring Juliet forth; her lord
 is come.
Nurse. She's dead, deceased: she's dead, alack
 the day!
Lady Capulet. Alack the day, she's dead, she's dead,
 she's dead!
Capulet. Ha, let me see her. Out, alas! She's cold,
Her blood is settled, and her joints are stiff:
Life and these lips have long been separated;

Death lies on her like an untimely frost
Upon the sweetest flower of all the field.

30 *Nurse.* O lamentable day!
    Lady Capulet.   O woeful time!
    Capulet. Death, that hath ta'en her hence to make
        me wail,
Ties up my tongue and will not let me speak.

    '*Enter* FRIAR *and the* COUNTY' *with Musicians*

    Friar. Come, is the bride ready to go to church?
    Capulet. Ready to go, but never to return.
O son, the night before thy wedding day
Hath Death lain with thy wife. There she lies,
Flower as she was, defloweréd by him.
Death is my son-in-law, Death is my heir;
My daughter he hath wedded! I will die
40 And leave him all; life, living, all is Death's.
    Paris. Have I thought long to see this morning's face,
And doth it give me such a sight as this?
    Lady Capulet. Accursed, unhappy, wretched,
        hateful day!
Most miserable hour that e'er time saw
In lasting labour of his pilgrimage!
But one, poor one, one poor and loving child,
But one thing to rejoice and solace in,
And cruel Death hath catched it from my sight!
    Nurse. O woe! O woeful, woeful, woeful day!
50 Most lamentable day, most woeful day
That ever, ever I did yet behold!
O day, O day, O day, O hateful day!
Never was seen so black a day as this.
O woeful day, O woeful day!
    Paris. Beguiled, divorcéd, wrongéd, spited, slain!
Most detestable Death, by thee beguiled,

By cruel, cruel thee quite overthrown!
O love! O life! Not life, but love in death!
  Capulet. Despised, distresséd, hated,
    martyred, killed!
Uncomfortable time, why cam'st thou now   60
To murder, murder our solemnity?
O child, O child! my soul, and not my child!
Dead art thou. Alack, my child is dead,
And with my child my joys are buriéd!
  Friar. Peace, ho, for shame! Confusion's cure
    lives not
In these confusions. Heaven and yourself
Had part in this fair maid; now heaven hath all,
And all the better is it for the maid.
Your part in her you could not keep from death,
But heaven keeps his part in eternal life.   70
The most you sought was her promotion,
For 'twas your heaven she should be advanced;
And weep ye now, seeing she is advanced
Above the clouds as high as heaven itself?
O, in this love you love your child so ill
That you run mad, seeing that she is well.
She's not well married that lives married long,
But she's best married that dies married young.
Dry up your tears and stick your rosemary
On this fair corse, and as the custom is,   80
All in her best array, bear her to church:
For though fond nature bids us all lament,
Yet nature's tears are reason's merriment.
  Capulet. All things that we ordainéd festival
Turn from their office to black funeral,
Our instruments to melancholy bells,
Our wedding cheer to a sad burial feast;
Our solemn hymns to sullen dirges change,

7   PSR&J

Our bridal flowers serve for a buried corse,
90 And all things change them to the contrary.
  Friar. Sir, go you in; and, madam, go
    with him;
And go, Sir Paris. Everyone prepare
To follow this fair corse unto her grave.
The heavens do lour upon you for some ill;
Move them no more by crossing their high will.
[*'all but the Nurse' and the Musicians 'go forth, casting
      rosemary upon her and shutting the curtains'*
  1 *Musician.* Faith, we may put up our pipes and
    be gone.
  Nurse. Honest good fellows, ah, put up, put up!
For well you know this is a pitiful case.
  1 *Musician.* Ay, by my troth, the case may
    be amended.   [*Nurse goes*

Enter PETER

100   *Peter.* Musicians, O musicians, 'Heart's ease',
'Heart's ease'! O, an you will have me live, play
'Heart's ease'.
  1 *Musician.* Why 'Heart's ease'?
  Peter. O musicians, because my heart itself plays
'My heart is full of woe'. O play me some merry dump
to comfort me.
  1 *Musician.* Not a dump we! 'Tis no time to play
now.
  Peter. You will not then?
110   1 *Musician.* No.
  Peter. I will then give it you soundly.
  1 *Musician.* What will you give us?
  Peter. No money, on my faith, but the gleek. I will
give you the minstrel.
  1 *Musician.* Then will I give you the serving-creature.

Peter. Then will I lay the serving-creature's dagger on your pate. I will carry no crotchets. I'll re you, I'll fa you. Do you note me?

1 *Musician.* An you re us and fa us, you note us.

2 *Musician.* Pray you put up your dagger, and put 120 out your wit.

Peter. Then have at you with my wit! I will dry-beat you with an iron wit, and put up my iron dagger. Answer me like men:

> 'When griping grief the heart doth wound,
>   And doleful dumps the mind oppress,
>   Then music with her silver sound—'

Why 'silver sound'? Why 'music with her silver sound'? What say you, Simon Catling?

1 *Musician.* Marry, sir, because silver hath a sweet 130 sound.

Peter. Pretty! What say you, Hugh Rebeck?

2 *Musician.* I say 'silver sound', because musicians sound for silver.

Peter. Pretty too! What say you, James Soundpost?

3 *Musician.* Faith, I know not what to say.

Peter. O, I cry you mercy! You are the singer. I will say for you. It is 'music with her silver sound', because musicians have no gold for sounding.

> 'Then music with her silver sound   140
>   With speedy help doth lend redress.'

[he goes

1 *Musician.* What a pestilent knave is this same!

2 *Musician.* Hang him, Jack! Come, we'll in here, tarry for the mourners, and stay dinner.

[they go also

[5. 1.]   *Mantua. A street with shops*

'*Enter* ROMEO'

Romeo. If I may trust the flattering truth of sleep,
My dreams presage some joyful news at hand.
My bosom's lord sits lightly in his throne,
And all this day an unaccustomed spirit
Lifts me above the ground with cheerful thoughts.
I dreamt my lady came and found me dead—
Strange dream that gives a dead man leave
        to think!—
And breathed such life with kisses in my lips
That I revived and was an emperor.
10 Ah me! how sweet is love itself possessed,
When but love's shadows are so rich in joy!

Enter BALTHASAR, *Romeo's man, booted*

News from Verona! How now, Balthasar?
Dost thou not bring me letters from the friar?
How doth my lady? Is my father well?
How fares my Juliet? That I ask again,
For nothing can be ill if she be well.
    Balthasar. Then she is well, and nothing can
        be ill.
Her body sleeps in Capel's monument,
And her immortal part with angels lives.
20 I saw her laid low in her kindred's vault,
And presently took post to tell it you.
O pardon me for bringing these ill news,
Since you did leave it for my office, sir.
    Romeo. Is it e'en so? Then I defy you, stars!
Thou know'st my lodging. Get me ink and paper,
And hire post-horses; I will hence tonight.

Balthasar. I do beseech you, sir, have patience.
Your looks are pale and wild and do import
Some misadventure.

Romeo.   Tush, thou art deceived.
Leave me, and do the thing I bid thee do.   30
Hast thou no letters to me from the friar?

Balthasar. No, my good lord.

Romeo.   No matter. Get thee gone,
And hire those horses; I'll be with thee straight.

                                    [*Balthasar goes*

Well, Juliet, I will lie with thee tonight.
Let's see for means. O mischief, thou art swift
To enter in the thoughts of desperate men!
I do remember an apothecary,
And hereabouts 'a dwells, which late I noted
In tatt'red weeds, with overwhelming brows,
Culling of simples. Meagre were his looks;   40
Sharp misery had worn him to the bones:
And in his needy shop a tortoise hung,
An alligator stuffed, and other skins
Of ill-shaped fishes; and about his shelves
A beggarly account of empty boxes,
Green earthen pots, bladders, and musty seeds,
Remnants of packthread, and old cakes of roses
Were thinly scattered, to make up a show.
Noting this penury, to myself I said,
'An if a man did need a poison now,   50
Whose sale is present death in Mantua,
Here lives a caitiff wretch would sell it him'.
O, this same thought did but forerun my need,
And this same needy man must sell it me.
As I remember, this should be the house.
Being holiday, the beggar's shop is shut.
What ho, apothecary!

Enter APOTHECARY

Apothecary.   Who calls so loud?

Romeo. Come hither, man. I see that thou art poor.
Hold, there is forty ducats; let me have
60 A dram of poison, such soon-speeding gear
As will disperse itself through all the veins
That the life-weary taker may fall dead,
And that the trunk may be discharged of breath
As violently as hasty powder fired
Doth hurry from the fatal cannon's womb.

Apothecary. Such mortal drugs I have, but
          Mantua's law
Is death to any he that utters them.

Romeo. Art thou so bare and full of wretchedness
And fear'st to die? Famine is in thy cheeks,
70 Need and oppression starveth in thy eyes,
Contempt and beggary hangs upon thy back:
The world is not thy friend, nor the world's law;
The world affords no law to make thee rich:
Then be not poor, but break it and take this.

Apothecary. My poverty but not my will consents.

Romeo. I pay thy poverty and not thy will.

Apothecary. [*giving a phial*] Put this in any liquid
          thing you will
And drink it off, and if you had the strength
Of twenty men it would dispatch you straight.

80 *Romeo.* There is thy gold—worse poison to
          men's souls,
Doing more murder in this loathsome world,
Than these poor compounds that thou mayst not sell.
I sell thee poison; thou hast sold me none.
Farewell; buy food and get thyself in flesh.

          [*Apothecary goes in*

Come, cordial and not poison, go with me
To Juliet's grave, for there must I use thee.

[he passes on

[5. 2.]   *Verona. Friar Lawrence's cell*

Enter Friar JOHN

Friar John. Holy Franciscan friar, brother, ho!

Enter Friar LAWRENCE

Friar Lawrence. This same should be the voice of
    Friar John.
Welcome from Mantua. What says Romeo?
Or, if his mind be writ, give me his letter.
    Friar John. Going to find a barefoot brother out,
One of our order, to associate me,
Here in this city visiting the sick,
And finding him, the searchers of the town,
Suspecting that we both were in a house
Where the infectious pestilence did reign,   10
Sealed up the doors, and would not let us forth,
So that my speed to Mantua there was stayed.
    Friar Lawrence. Who bare my letter then to Romeo?
    Friar John. I could not send it—here it is again—
Nor get a messenger to bring it thee,
So fearful were they of infection.
    Friar Lawrence. Unhappy fortune! By
        my brotherhood,
The letter was not nice, but full of charge,
Of dear import; and the neglecting it
May do much danger. Friar John, go hence,   20
Get me an iron crow and bring it straight
Unto my cell.

Friar John. Brother, I'll go and bring it thee. *[goes*
Friar Lawrence. Now must I to the monument alone.
Within this three hours will fair Juliet wake.
She will beshrew me much that Romeo
Hath had no notice of these accidents;
But I will write again to Mantua,
And keep her at my cell till Romeo come.
30 Poor living corse, closed in a dead man's tomb!

           [he goes

[5. 3.] *Verona. A churchyard; in it the*
     monument of the Capulets

  '*Enter* PARIS *and his* PAGE', *bearing*
     flowers and a torch

Paris. Give me thy torch, boy. Hence, and
  stand aloof.
Yet put it out, for I would not be seen.
Under yond yew-trees lay thee all along,
Holding thine ear close to the hollow ground;
So shall no foot upon the churchyard tread,
Being loose, unfirm with digging up of graves,
But thou shalt hear it. Whistle then to me
As signal that thou hear'st some thing approach.
Give me those flowers. Do as I bid thee; go.
10 (*Page.* I am almost afraid to stand alone
Here in the churchyard, yet I will adventure.

           [retires

Paris. Sweet flower, with flowers thy bridal bed
  I strew—
O woe, thy canopy is dust and stones!—
Which with sweet water nightly I will dew,
Or, wanting that, with tears distilled by moans.

The obsequies that I for thee will keep
Nightly shall be to strew thy grave and weep.
                              [*Page whistles*
The boy gives warning something doth approach.
What curséd foot wanders this way tonight
To cross my obsequies and true love's rite?   20
What, with a torch? Muffle me, night, awhile.
                              [*retires*

'*Enter* ROMEO *and* BALTHASAR, *with a torch,*
a mattock, and a crow of iron'

  Romeo. Give me that mattock and the wrenching iron.
Hold, take this letter. Early in the morning
See thou deliver it to my lord and father.
Give me the light. Upon thy life I charge thee,
Whate'er thou hear'st or seest, stand all aloof
And do not interrupt me in my course.
Why I descend into this bed of death
Is partly to behold my lady's face,
But chiefly to take thence from her dead finger   30
A precious ring, a ring that I must use
In dear employment. Therefore hence, be gone.
But if thou, jealous, dost return to pry
In what I farther shall intend to do,
By heaven, I will tear thee joint by joint
And strew this hungry churchyard with thy limbs.
The time and my intents are savage-wild,
More fierce and more inexorable far
Than empty tigers or the roaring sea.
  Balthasar. I will be gone, sir, and not trouble ye.   40
  Romeo. So shalt thou show me friendship. Take
        thou that;   [*gives money*
Live and be prosperous; and farewell, good fellow.
  (*Balthasar.* For all this same, I'll hide me hereabout.

His looks I fear, and his intents I doubt.   [*retires*

  Romeo. Thou detestable maw, thou womb of death,

Gorged with the dearest morsel of the earth,

Thus I enforce thy rotten jaws to open,

                             [*begins to open the tomb*

And in despite I'll cram thee with more food.

  (*Paris*. This is that banished haughty Montague

50 That murd'red my love's cousin—with which grief

It is supposéd the fair creature died—

And here is come to do some villainous shame

To the dead bodies: I will apprehend him.—

                             [*comes forward*

Stop thy unhallowed toil, vile Montague!

Can vengeance be pursued further than death?

Condemnéd villain, I do apprehend thee.

Obey, and go with me, for thou must die.

  Romeo. I must indeed, and therefore came I hither.

Good gentle youth, tempt not a desp'rate man.

60 Fly hence and leave me. Think upon these gone;

Let them affright thee. I beseech thee, youth,

Put not another sin upon my head

By urging me to fury. O be gone!

By heaven, I love thee better than myself,

For I come hither armed against myself.

Stay not, be gone. Live, and hereafter say

A madman's mercy bid thee run away.

  Paris. I do defy thy conjuration,

And apprehend thee for a felon here.

70 *Romeo*. Wilt thou provoke me? Then have at thee, boy!

                             [*they fight*

  Page. O Lord, they fight! I will go call the watch.

                             [*runs off*

  Paris. O, I am slain! [*falls*] If thou be merciful,

Open the tomb, lay me with Juliet.   [*dies*

Romeo. In faith, I will. Let me peruse this face.
Mercutio's kinsman, noble County Paris!
What said my man when my betosséd soul
Did not attend him as we rode? I think
He told me Paris should have married Juliet.
Said he not so? Or did I dream it so?
Or am I mad, hearing him talk of Juliet,   80
To think it was so? O give me thy hand,
One writ with me in sour misfortune's book!
I'll bury thee in a triumphant grave.
A grave? O no!—a lanthorn, slaught'red youth:
For here lies Juliet, and her beauty makes
This vault a feasting presence full of light.
Dead, lie thou there, by a dead man interred.
                    [*lays Paris within the tomb*
How oft when men are at the point of death
Have they been merry, which their keepers call
A light'ning before death! O, how may I   90
Call this a light'ning? O my love, my wife!
Death, that hath sucked the honey of thy breath,
Hath had no power yet upon thy beauty.
Thou art not conquered; beauty's ensign yet
Is crimson in thy lips and in thy cheeks,
And death's pale flag is not advancéd there.
Tybalt, liest thou there in thy bloody sheet?
O, what more favour can I do to thee
Than with that hand that cut thy youth in twain
To sunder his that was thine enemy?   100
Forgive me, cousin! Ah, dear Juliet,
Why art thou yet so fair? Shall I believe
That unsubstantial Death is amorous,
And that the lean abhorréd monster keeps
Thee here in dark to be his paramour?
For fear of that I still will stay with thee,

And never from this palace of dim night
Depart again. Here, here will I remain
With worms that are thy chambermaids. O, here
110 Will I set up my everlasting rest,
And shake the yoke of inauspicious stars
From this world-wearied flesh. Eyes, look your last!
Arms, take your last embrace! and lips, O you,
The doors of breath, seal with a righteous kiss
A dateless bargain to engrossing Death!
Come, bitter conduct; come, unsavoury guide!
Thou desperate pilot, now at once run on
The dashing rocks thy seasick weary bark!
Here's to my love! [*drinks*] O true apothecary!
120 Thy drugs are quick. Thus with a kiss I die.   [*dies*

'*Enter Friar*' LAWRENCE '*with lanthorn,
crow, and spade*'

Friar. Saint Francis be my speed! how oft tonight
Have my old feet stumbled at graves! Who's there?
Balthasar. Here's one, a friend, and one that knows
you well.
Friar. Bliss be upon you! Tell me, good my friend,
What torch is yond that vainly lends his light
To grubs and eyeless skulls? As I discern,
It burneth in the Capels' monument.
Balthasar. It doth so, holy sir; and there's
my master,
One that you love.
     Friar.   Who is it?
     Balthasar.   Romeo.
130 *Friar.* How long hath he been there?
     Balthasar. ·   .   Full half an hour.
     Friar. Go with me to the vault.
     Balthasar.   I dare not, sir.

My master knows not but I am gone hence,
And fearfully did menace me with death
If I did stay to look on his intents.
  Friar. Stay then; I'll go alone. Fear comes upon me.
O, much I fear some ill unthrifty thing.
  Balthasar. As I did sleep under this yew-tree here,
I dreamt my master and another fought,
And that my master slew him.
  Friar.   Romeo!   [*advances*
Alack, alack, what blood is this which stains   140
The stony entrance of this sepulchre?
What mean these masterless and gory swords
To lie discoloured by this place of peace?
                                        [*enters the tomb*
Romeo! O, pale! Who else? What, Paris too?
And steeped in blood? Ah, what an unkind hour
Is guilty of this lamentable chance!
The lady stirs.   [*Juliet wakes*
  Juliet. O comfortable friar, where is my lord?
I do remember well where I should be,
And there I am. Where is my Romeo? [*voices afar off* 150
  Friar. I hear some noise, lady. Come from that nest
Of death, contagion, and unnatural sleep.
A greater power than we can contradict
Hath thwarted our intents. Come, come away.
Thy husband in thy bosom there lies dead:
And Paris too. Come, I'll dispose of thee
Among a sisterhood of holy nuns.
Stay not to question, for the watch is coming.
Come, go, good Juliet; I dare no longer stay.
  Juliet. Go, get thee hence, for I will not away.   160
                                        [*he goes*
What's here? A cup, closed in my true love's hand?
Poison, I see, hath been his timeless end,

O churl! drunk all, and left no friendly drop
To help me after? I will kiss thy lips.
Haply some poison yet doth hang on them
To make me die with a restorative.   [*kisses him*
Thy lips are warm!

*The Page of Paris enters the graveyard
with Watch*

1 *Watchman.* Lead, boy. Which way?

Juliet. Yea, noise? Then I'll be brief. O happy
        dagger,   [*snatching Romeo's dagger*
170 This is thy sheath [*stabs herself*]; there rest, and let
        me die.   [*falls on Romeo's body and dies*

Page. This is the place, there where the torch
        doth burn.

1 *Watchman.* The ground is bloody. Search about
        the churchyard.
Go, some of you; whoe'er you find attach.
                                [*some Watchmen depart*
Pitiful sight! Here lies the County slain:
And Juliet bleeding, warm and newly dead,
Who here hath lain this two days buriéd.
Go tell the Prince; run to the Capulets;
Raise up the Montagues; some others search.
                                [*other Watchmen depart*
We see the ground whereon these woes do lie,
180 But the true ground of all these piteous woes
We cannot without circumstance descry.

Re-enter some of the Watch, with BALTHASAR

2 *Watchman.* Here's Romeo's man; we found him in
        the churchyard.

1 *Watchman.* Hold him in safety till the Prince
        come hither.

Re-enter another Watchman, with Friar LAWRENCE

3 *Watchman.* Here is a friar that trembles, sighs,
    and weeps.
We took this mattock and this spade from him
As he was coming from this churchyard's side.
  1 *Watchman.* A great suspicion! Stay the friar too.

      'Enter the Prince' and attendants

Prince. What misadventure is so early up,
That calls our person from our morning rest?

      Enter CAPULET *and his wife*

Capulet. What should it be that is so
    shrieked abroad?   190
Lady Capulet. O, the people in the street
    cry 'Romeo',
Some 'Juliet', and some 'Paris', and all run
With open outcry toward our monument.
  Prince. What fear is this which startles in our ears?
  1 *Watchman.* Sovereign, here lies the County
    Paris slain;
And Romeo dead; and Juliet, dead before,
Warm and new killed.
  Prince. Search, seek, and know how this foul
    murder comes.
  1 *Watchman.* Here is a friar, and slaughtered
    Romeo's man,
With instruments upon them fit to open   200
These dead men's tombs.
  Capulet. O heaven! O wife, look how our
    daughter bleeds!
This dagger hath mista'en, for, lo, his house
Is empty on the back of Montague,

And it mis-sheathéd in my daughter's bosom.

Lady Capulet. O me! this sight of death is as a bell
That warns my old age to a sepulchre.

'*Enter* MONTAGUE'

Prince. Come Montague; for thou art early up
To see thy son and heir more early down.

210 *Montague.* Alas, my liege, my wife is dead tonight;
Grief of my son's exile hath stopped her breath.
What further woe conspires against mine age?

Prince. Look and thou shalt see.

Montague. O thou untaught! what manners is
    in this,
To press before thy father to a grave?

Prince. Seal up the mouth of outrage for a while,
Till we can clear these ambiguities,
And know their spring, their head, their true descent;
And then will I be general of your woes,
220 And lead you even to death. Meantime forbear,
And let mischance be slave to patience.
Bring forth the parties of suspicion.

> [*Watchmen bring forward Friar Lawrence
>   and Balthasar*

Friar. I am the greatest; able to do least,
Yet most suspected, as the time and place
Doth make against me, of this direful murder:
And here I stand both to impeach and purge
Myself condemnéd and myself excused.

Prince. Then say at once what thou dost know
    in this.

Friar. I will be brief, for my short date of breath
230 Is not so long as is a tedious tale.
Romeo there dead was husband to that Juliet;
And she, there dead, that Romeo's faithful wife.

I married them; and their stol'n marriage day
Was Tybalt's doomsday, whose untimely death
Banished the new-made bridegroom from this city;
For whom, and not for Tybalt, Juliet pined.
You, to remove that siege of grief from her,
Betrothed and would have married her perforce
To County Paris. Then comes she to me,
And with wild looks bid me devise some mean   240
To rid her from this second marriage,
Or in my cell there would she kill herself.
Then gave I her (so tutored by my art)
A sleeping potion; which so took effect
As I intended, for it wrought on her
The form of death. Meantime I writ to Romeo
That he should hither come as this dire night
To help to take her from her borrowed grave,
Being the time the potion's force should cease.
But he which bore my letter, Friar John,   250
Was stayed by accident, and yesternight
Returned my letter back. Then all alone
At the prefixéd hour of her waking
Came I to take her from her kindred's vault,
Meaning to keep her closely at my cell
Till I conveniently could send to Romeo.
But when I came, some minute ere the time
Of her awakening, here untimely lay
The noble Paris and true Romeo dead.
She wakes; and I entreated her come forth,   260
And bear this work of heaven with patience;
But then a noise did scare me from the tomb,
And she, too desperate, would not go with me,
But, as it seems, did violence on herself.
All this I know; and to the marriage
Her nurse is privy: and if aught in this

Miscarried by my fault, let my old life
Be sacrificed, some hour before his time,
Unto the rigour of severest law.

270   *Prince.* We still have known thee for a holy man.
Where's Romeo's man? What can he say to this?
 Balthasar. I brought my master news of
  Juliet's death,
And then in post he came from Mantua
To this same place, to this same monument.
This letter he early bid me give his father,
And threat'ned me with death, going in the vault,
If I departed not and left him there.
 Prince. Give me the letter; I will look on it.
Where is the County's page, that raised the watch?
      [*Page comes forward*
280 Sirrah, what made your master in this place?
 Page. He came with flowers to strew his
  lady's grave,
And bid me stand aloof, and so I did.
Anon comes one with light to ope the tomb,
And by and by my master drew on him,
And then I ran away to call the watch.
 Prince. This letter doth make good the
  friar's words,
Their course of love, the tidings of her death;
And here he writes that he did buy a poison
Of a poor pothecary, and therewithal
290 Came to this vault to die, and lie with Juliet.
Where be these enemies? Capulet, Montague?
See what a scourge is laid upon your hate,
That heaven finds means to kill your joys with love!
And I, for winking at your discords too,
Have lost a brace of kinsmen. All are punished.
 Capulet. O brother Montague, give me thy hand.

This is my daughter's jointure, for no more
Can I demand.

   Montague.   But I can give thee more;
For I will raise her statue in pure gold,
That, whiles Verona by that name is known,   300
There shall no figure at such rate be set
As that of true and faithful Juliet.

   Capulet. As rich shall Romeo's by his lady's lie—
Poor sacrifices of our enmity!

   Prince. A glooming peace this morning with
      it brings;
   The sun for sorrow will not show his head.
Go hence, to have more talk of these sad things.
   Some shall be pardoned, and some punishéd;
For never was a story of more woe
Than this of Juliet and her Romeo.   *[they go* 310

GLOSSARY

Note. Where a pun or quibble is intended, the meanings are distinguished as (*a*) and (*b*)

'A (for 'ha'), he; 1. 3. 41; 1. 4. 80; 1. 5. 66; 2. 4. 114, 145, 146; 5. 1. 38

ABROACH, afoot; 1. 1. 103

ABROAD, (i) out of doors; 1. 1. 119; 3. 1. 2; (ii) far and wide; 5. 3. 190

ABUSE (sb.), (i) misuse; 2. 3. 20; (ii) offence, crime; 3. 1. 192

ABUSE (vb.), mar, disfigure; 4. 1. 29

ACCENT, manner of speech; 2. 4. 29

ACCIDENT, event; 5. 2. 26

ACCORDING, consenting; 1.2.19

ACCOUNT, (i) reckoning; 1. 5. 118; (ii) store, number; 5. 1. 45

ACTED, put into (physical) action, consummated; 3. 2. 16

ADVANCE, raise, lift up; 2. 3. 5; 4. 5. 72 (in social standing); 4. 5. 73; 5. 3. 96

ADVISE, reflect, consider; 3. 5. 190

AFFECTING, affected; 2. 4. 28

AFFECTION, (i) inclination, feeling; 1. 1. 125, 146; (ii) love; 2 Prol. 2; (iii) passion, emotion, natural feeling; 2. 5. 12; (iv) partiality, biased feeling; 3. 1. 176

AFFORD, 'manage to give, spare' (O.E.D. 4 a); 3. 1. 59

AFFRAY, startle, scare; 3. 5. 33

AFORE ME, by my soul; 3. 4. 34

AGATE-STONE, tiny figure cut out in an agate set in a seal-ring (cf. *Ado*, 3. 1. 65; *2 Hen. IV*, 1. 2. 16); 1. 4. 55

AIM, (*a*) direct a weapon, (*b*) guess; 1. 1. 204

ALLA STOCCATA (Ital.), the thrust technique (v. note; cf. à la=after the manner of); 3. 1. 73

ALLIANCE, marriage; 2. 3. 91

ALLOW, grant; 2. 3. 86

ALLY, kinsman; 3. 1. 108

ALOOF, at a distance; 5. 3. 1, 26, 282

AMAZE, bewilder, astonish, 3. 1. 133; 3. 3. 114

AMBIGUITY, uncertainty; 5. 3. 217

AMBLING, dancing (contemptuous term); 1. 4. 11

AMBUSCADO, ambush; 1. 4. 84

AMERCE, punish by fining; 3. 1. 189

ANATOMY, bodily frame (contemptuous term); 3. 3. 106

ANON, (i) in a little while, soon; 1. 4. 85; 5. 3. 283; (ii) (as answer to a call) 'coming!'; 1. 5. 143; 2. 2. 137, 150; (iii) (do.) 'at your service!'; 2. 4. 101, 208

ANTIC, grotesque; 1. 5. 56; 2. 4. 28

APT TO, UNTO, ready for; 3.
1. 40; 3. 3. 157

AQUA VITAE, any form of
ardent spirits; 3. 2. 88; 4. 5.
16

ARGUE, betoken, indicate; 2. 3.
33

ARGUMENT, subject of discus-
sion; 2. 4. 97

ART, skill acquired by learning
or experience (as opposed to
'nature'); 2. 4. 88; 4. 1. 64;
5. 3. 243

As, as on; 5. 3. 247

ASPIRE (trans.), mount up to;
3. 1. 116

ASSOCIATE, accompany; 5. 2. 6

ATOMI, tiny creatures; 1. 4. 57

ATTACH, arrest; 5. 3. 173

AURORA, name of classical goddess of dawn; 1. 1. 135

BACHELOR, young gentleman;
1. 5. 112

BAKE, cake together; 1. 4. 90

BAKED MEATS, pies and other
pastry; 4. 4. 5

BALEFUL, deadly; 2. 3. 8

BANDY, (i) strike a ball to and
fro (a term of tennis, or
bandy, once a form of tennis); 2. 5. 14; (ii) give and
take (blows); 3. 1. 88

BANKROUT (Ital. 'banca rotta',
Fr. 'banqueroute'), bank-
rupt; fig. one who has lost
all; 3. 2. 57

BANQUET, dessert of sweetmeats, fruit and wine (v.
Shrew, G.); 1. 5. 122

BATE (vb.), flutter. Of a hawk
trying to fly from its tamer's
wrist; 3. 2. 14

BAUBLE, (a) short stick, sur-
mounted by carved head,
carried by court fool, (b)
penis (cf. *All's Well*, G.);
2. 4. 90

BAWD, (a) procuress, (b) In
dial., North Midland = hare;
2. 4. 125

BECOMED, befitting, becoming;
4. 2. 26

BEDECK, adorn; 3. 3. 125

BEETLE-BROWS, overhanging
eyebrows; 1. 4. 32

BEGUILED, cheated; (i) pre-
vented from fulfilling proper
function; 3. 2. 132; (ii) dis-
appointed as regards hopes
for the future; 4. 5. 55,
56

BEHOVEFUL, needful, advanta-
geous; 4. 3. 8

BENEDICITE. The 2nd pers. pl.
imperative of Lat. vb.
'benedico' = 'Bless you'—a
salutation, or an exclamation of surprise; 2. 3. 31

BENT, inclination (of the
mind); 2. 2. 143

BESEEMING, seemly, decorous;
1. 1. 92

BESHREW, curse; 2. 5. 51; 3. 5.
221, 227; 5. 2. 26

BETOSSÉD, agitated; 5. 3. 76

BIDE, endure; 1. 1. 212

BILL, 'an obsolete weapon
varying in form from a
simple concave blade with a
long wooden handle, to
a kind of concave axe with
a spike at the back and its
shaft terminating in a spear-
head; a halberd.' (O.E.D.
sb.[1], 2); 1. 1. 72

BIRD, maiden (cf. *Cymb.* 4. 2.
197; O.E.D. 1 d); 2. . 5.
74

BIRTH, nature; 2. 3. 20

BITE, (i) 'bite the thumb at'=insult, 'threaten or defy by putting the thumb-nail into the mouth, and with a jerk (from the upper teeth) make it to knack' (O.E.D., cited from Cotgrave); 1. 1. 42–50; (ii) 'bite one by the ear' (i.e. as a sign of fondness, 'to caress fondly' (O.E.D.)); 2. 4. 77

BLAZE, proclaim, make known publicly; 3. 3. 151

BLAZON, describe fitly (lit. heraldic term); 2. 6. 26

BOOK, (i) 'without book'=by rote; 1. 2. 60; 'without-book'=recited by heart; 1. 4. 7; (ii) 'by th' book'—O.E.D. gives 'formally, in set phrase', but prob.=according to a book of rules, as if you had learned pre-scribed rules from a text-book or breviary (cf. 3. 1. 101, n.); 1. 5. 110

BOUT, round, turn, at any kind of exercise (here dancing); 1. 5. 18

BOW-BOY, boy archer (Cupid); 2. 4. 16

BOWER, embower; 3. 2. 81

BOY, (i) familiar address to fellow-servant; 1. 5. 11, 15; (ii) reproving term for re-calcitrant junior; 1. 5. 77, 83; (iii) insulting term ap-plied by one young enemy to another; 3. 1. 129; 5. 3. 70

BRAIN, 'I do bear a brain'=I have a fine memory; 1. 3. 30

BRAVE, fine, splendid, noble; 3. 1. 115

BREACHES, i.e. in the walls of besieged towns; 1. 4. 84

BRIEF (adv.), quickly; 3. 3. 173

BROAD, (a) 'plain, evident' (Schmidt; cf. O.E.D. 5), (b) indecent; 2. 4. 85

BUCKLER, small round shield; 1. 1. head S.D.

BURDEN, weight (a) of toil, (b) of a husband; 2. 5. 76

BURN DAYLIGHT, waste time (cf. Tilley, D 123); 1. 4. 43

BUTT-SHAFT, 'unbarbed arrow used in shooting at the butts' (O.E.D.), ludicrously applied to Cupid's dart (cf. L.L.L. 1. 2. 168); 2. 4. 16

BY AND BY, very soon, shortly; 2. 2. 151; 3. 1. 169; 3. 3. 77; 3. 4. 35; 5. 3. 284

CAGE, 'anything resembling a cage in structure or pur-pose' (O.E.D. 4), in this case a basket; 2. 3. 7

CAITIFF, 'expressing commis-eration: a wretched miser-able person, a poor wretch, one in a piteous case' (O.E.D. 2), used as adj.; 5. 1. 52

CAKE OF ROSES or ROSE-CAKE, 'a preparation of rose-petals in the form of a cake, used as a perfume' (O.E.D.); 5. 1. 47

CALL IN QUESTION, 'make the object of thought or of notice' (K.); 1. 1. 228

CANDLE-HOLDER, an attendant who lights others in a cere-mony at night (cf. O.E.D.); 1. 4. 38

CANKER, worm that destroys plants; 2. 3. 30

CANKERED, (i) of weapons, 'cankered with peace'=

rusted, corroded, through disuse; 1. 1. 94; (ii) of persons or sentiments— malignant; 1. 1. 94

CAREFUL, concerned for some-one's welfare; 3. 5. 107

CARELESSLY, with indifference; 'held him carelessly'=did not value him highly; 3. 4. 25

CARRIAGE, power of bearing a weight (v. *burden*), with quibble on bodily deportment and/or moral character; 1. 4. 94

CARRION, applied in contempt to a living person, as being no better than a decaying corpse; 3. 5. 156

CARRY, endure, put up with (O.E.D. 39); 4. 5. 117

CARRY COALS, 'do dirty or degrading work', hence 'submit to humiliation or insult' at the hands of one's enemies (v. O.E.D. 'coal', 12, and Tilley, C 464); 1. 1. 1

CASE, (i) mask; 1. 4. 29; (ii) (*a*) state of affairs, (*b*) case for musical instruments (or perhaps set of instruments; cf. *Hen. V*, 3. 2. 4); 4. 5. 99

CAST BY, throw aside; 1. 1. 92

CATLING, 'a small lute-string made of catgut' (Steevens), as a personal name; 4. 5. 122

CHANGE (sb.), succession, passage; 1. 2. 9

CHAPLESS, without lower jaw; 4. 1. 83

CHARGE, importance, weight; 5. 2. 18

CHARM, (*a*) magic spell, (*b*) attractive quality; 2. Prol. 6

CHARNEL HOUSE, 'a vault or small building attached to a church and used as a depository for such skulls and bones as came to light in digging new graves' (K.); 4. 1. 81

CHASTE, unmarried; 1. 1. 216

CHECK'RING, diversifying with a different colour, variegating; 2. 3. 2

CHEER, fare, provisions, viands; 4. 5. 87

CHEVERIL, kid leather, capable of being stretched (cf. *Tw. Nt.* G.); 2. 4. 82

CHINKS, coins (from the sound made by their striking against one another); 'have the chinks'=have plenty of money; 1. 5. 117

CHOP-LOGIC, sophistical argumentation ('chop'='bandy', not 'mince'); 3. 5. 149

CHORUS, Presenter or Prologue, to 'make plain' the action (cf. *V.A.* 360; Creizenach, pp. 276, 389); acts 1 and 2

CHURL, niggard, stingy person; 5. 3. 163

CIRCLE, (*a*) magic ring, circular area within which a conjuror recited his spells, (*b*) female pudenda; 2. 1. 24

CIRCUMSTANCE, details, detailed information; 2. 5. 36; 5. 3. 181

CIVIL, (i) belonging to citizens; Prol. 4; (ii) occurring among fellow-citizens; 1. 1. 88; (iii) seemly, decorous, in attire (and perh. behaviour); 3. 2. 10

CLASP, metal clasp to keep a book shut (with quibble on 'embrace of a lover'), 1. 3. 93

CLOSE (adj.), (i) reserved, private; 1. 1. 148; 2. 2. 188; (ii) shut fast, *or* concealing; 3. 2. 5

CLOSE (adv.), at close quarters, hand to hand; 1. 1. 106

CLOSE (vb.), (i) enclose; 1. 4. 110; 5. 2. 29; 5. 3. 161; (ii) join; 2. 6. 6.

CLOSELY, secretly; 5. 3. 255

CLOSET, private room; 4. 2. 33

CLOUT, rag, piece of cloth (cf. *dishclout*); 2. 4. 198

CLUBS, 'the regular weapon of the London journeyman and apprentices. The cry "Clubs!" was the citizens' watchword, whether in raising a riot or [as here] in rallying to keep the peace' (K.; cf. O.E.D. 1 c); 1. 1. 72

COCK-A-HOOP, 'set cock-a-hoop'='cast off all restraint, become reckless' or 'give a loose to all disorder, set all by the ears' (O.E.D.). Origin obscure; 1. 5. 81

COCKATRICE, mythical creature hatched from a cock's egg by a serpent, able to kill with its breath or by a look, also called 'basilisk'; 3. 2. 47

COIL, fuss; 2. 5. 65

COLDLY, coolly, calmly; 3. 1. 51

COLLAR, hangman's halter (but O.E.D. queries), with quibble on 'choler'; 1. 1. 5

COLLIER, 'one who carries coals for sale', 'often used with allusion to the dirtiness of the trade in coal, or the evil repute of the collier for cheating' (O.E.D. 2 and 3); 1. 1. 2

COMBINE, (i) 'all combined'='everything has been brought into harmonious union' (K.); 2. 3. 60; (ii) unite; 2. 3. 60

COME ABOUT, turn out to be true; 1. 3. 46

COME NEAR, affect intimately; 'touch closely' (O.E.D.); 1. 5. 21

COME UP (v. *marry come up*); 2. 5. 62

COMES WELL, is welcome; 1. 5. 30

COMFORTABLE, comfort-giving, supporting; 5. 3. 148

COMMISSION, a delegated authority for the performance of a judicial function (O.E.D. 2); 4. 1. 64

COMMON, (i) public, 1. 1. 101; (ii), ordinary; 1. 4. 18

COMPLAIN, utter laments, express grief, 'address pathetic words of love' (K.); 2. Prol. 7

COMPLIMENT (early edd. 'complement'), formal civility; 2. 2. 89; 2. 4. 20

CONCEIT, thoughts, imagination; 2. 6. 30 (v. note); 4. 3. 37

CONCEIVE, understand; 2. 4. 48

CONDUCT, (i) conductor, guide; 3. 1. 123; 5. 3. 116; (ii) guidance; 3. 3. 131

CONDUIT, fountain, 'often in the form of a human figure (hence allusively)' (On.).

Several in London in Sh.'s day; 3. 5. 129

CONFIDENCE, blunder for 'conference'; 2. 4. 122

CONFOUND, destroy; 2. 6. 13

CONFUSION, (i) calamity, disaster (K.); 4. 5. 65; (ii) (plur.) disorderly behaviour, lamenting commotions; 4.5. 66

CONJURATION, solemn appeal; 5. 3. 68

CONJURE, utter magical words to summon up a spirit; 2. 1. 6, 16, 17, 29; 'conjure down'=dismiss by magical words (with indelicate quibble); 2. 1. 26

CONSORT (intrans.), (i) associate; 2. 1. 31; 3. 1. 44; (ii) (with quibble on (i)) 'combine in musical harmony; play, sing or sound together' (O.E.D. 7); 3. 1. 45, 48; (trans.), attend, accompany; 3. 1. 129

CONTAGION, poisonous influence; 5. 3. 152

CONTENT, (a) pleasure, satisfaction, (b) 'contents'; 1. 3. 85

CONTRADICT, oppose; 5. 3. 153

CONTRARY (vb.), oppose; 1. 5. 85

CONVERT, change, be changed; 1. 5. 92

CONVOY, 'a conducting medium, channel, way, or path' (O.E.D. sb. 9). Quibbling on the nautical sense; 2. 4. 184

COPE WITH, encounter, engage, (O.E.D. 2); 4. 1. 75

CORDIAL, stimulant for the heart; exhilarating, restora-

tive, or comforting drink; 5. 1. 85

CORSE, corpse; 3. 2. 54, 128; 4. 5. 80, 89, 93; 5. 2. 29

COT-QUEAN, lit. housewife of a cot or labourer's hut; but 'to play the cot-quean' was said of a man who meddled with matters properly a housewife's concern. (Cf. O.E.D. 1, 3); 4. 4. 6

COUNSEL (sb.), (i) 'good counsel'=effective plan resulting from deliberation or consultation; 1. 1. 141; (ii) private talk; 1. 3. 10; 2. 2. 53; (iii) advice 2. 2. 81; 3. 3. 160; 4. 1. 61; (iv) 'keep counsel'= maintain secrecy; 2. 4. 190

COUNSEL (vb.), advise; 3. 5. 208

COUNSELLOR, secret advisor, confidant(e); 1. 1. 146; 3. 5. 239

COUNT (sb.), reckoning; 1. 3. 72; 3. 5. 46

COUNT (vb.), (i) reckon; 2. 6. 32; (ii) consider; 3. 5. 143; 4. 1. 9

COUNTERVAIL, equal, counterbalance; 2. 6. 4

COUNTY, title of nobility, Count; 1. 2. head S.D., and *passim*

COURSE, (i) (a) voyage, (b) life; 1. 4. 112; (ii) line of action, method or procedure; 4. 1. 5; 5. 3. 27; (iii) 'their course of love'=the progress of their love; 5. 3. 287

COURT-CUPBOARD, 'movable sideboard or cabinet used to display plate, etc.' (O.E.D.); 1. 5. 7

COURTSHIP, 'the state be-
fitting a court or courtier'
(O.E.D. 2), with quibble on
'courting, wooing'? (O.E.D.
6); (cf. *A.Y.L.* 3. 2. 340);
3. 3. 34

COUSIN, used in full, or ab-
breviated Coz, *passim* in ord.
mod. sense; but can indicate
any 'collateral relative more
distant than a brother or
sister' (O.E.D.), and =
nephew at 1. 5. 65; 3. 1.
145, 149

COVER, (i) binding of a book.
Quibbling on law-French
feme couvert=married woman (O.E.D. 'feme'); 1.
3. 89; (ii) hood of vehicle; 1.
4. 63

COVERT, concealment, shelter;
1. 1. 124

CROSS (adj.), perverse; 4. 3. 5

CROSS (vb.), go counter to,
interfere with; 4. 5. 95; 5.
3. 20

CROTCHET, (*a*) a note in music,
(*b*) silly notion (same quibble in *Ado*, 2. 3. 55); 4. 5.
117

CROW, crowbar; 5. 2. 21; 5. 3.
120 S.D.

CROW-KEEPER, boy with bow
and arrows, employed to pro-
tect a cornfield from crows;
1. 4. 6

CRUSH, 'crack', drink, quaff;
1. 2. 83

CRY, (i) 'cry a match'=
'claim the match as mine;
claim the victory' (K.); 2.
4. 70; (ii) 'cry mercy'=
beg pardon; 4. 5. 137; (iii)
'cry on'=exclaim against;
3. 3. 101

CUNNING (adj.), skilful; 4. 2. 2

CUNNING (sb.), artfulness; 2. 2.
101

CURE (intrans.), be cured; 1. 2.
49

CURFEW BELL. Orig. bell rung
in evening to indicate time
when domestic fires were to
be extinguished or covered
over (Fr. 'couvre feu'); but
also, as here, a bell rung at
3 or 4 a.m. (v. O.E.D.
'curfew' 1c); 4. 4. 4

CURIOUS, carefully observant;
1. 4. 31

CYNTHIA, the moon personified
as a goddess; 3. 5. 20

DAINTY (sb.), fastidiousness;
hence 'make dainty'=be
chary or loth; 1. 5. 20

DANGER, harm, damage; 5. 2. 20

DARE, (*a*) show courage, (*b*)
challenge; 2. 4. 12

DATE, duration, term of exis-
tence; 1. 4. 3, 108; 5. 3. 229

DATELESS, without term, end-
less; 5. 3. 115

DEAR, (i) valuable; 1. 5. 47;
3. 1. 182; (ii) hard, grievous; 1. 5. 118; (iii) fond,
affectionate; 2. 2. 115; 2. 3.
57; 3. 3. 128; (iv) fortunate,
happy; 2. 2. 189; (v) '? rare,
unusual, or ? loving, kind'
(O.E.D.), or great ('empha-
sizing' word) (K.); 3. 3. 28;
(vi) important, momentous;
5. 2. 19; 5. 3. 32

DEATH-MARKED, marked out
by Fate for death; Prol. 9

DEBT (fig.), 'someone's debt'
=at someone's mercy. (Cf.
O.E.D. 'debt' 20; 'danger'
1); 1. 5. 118

DEFENCE, means of defence, arms or armour; 3. 3. 134

DEFY, (i) challenge a person or power to do the worst; 5. 1. 24; (ii) reject; 5. 3. 68

DEMESNES, (i) regions; 2. 1. 20; (ii) estates; 3. 5. 180

DENY, (i) refuse; 1. 1. 156; 1. 5. 20; (ii) disown; 2. 2. 34

DESCENT, source, origin; 5. 3. 218

DESPERATE, (i) violently reckless; 3. 3. 108; 5. 3. 117, 263; (ii) bold, rash; 3. 4. 12

DESPISED, (i) despicable, 1. 4. 110; 3. 2. 77; (ii) 'hateful' (Schmidt); 4. 5. 59

DEVISE, (i) contrive, arrange; 2. 4. 173; 5. 3. 240; (ii) imagine, conceive, guess; 3. 1. 68

DEW-DROPPING, 'rainy' (Schmidt); 1. 4. 103

DIAL, clock; 2. 4. 109

DIAN, Diana, Latin goddess, early identified with the Greek Artemis, virgin huntress, regarded as a symbol of chastity, celibacy; 1. 1. 208

DIDO, Queen of Carthage, who slew herself when Aeneas deserted her (Virgil, *Aeneid*, iv); 2. 4. 41

DIFFERENT, 'opposed, hostile', (K.); 1. 5. 90

DIGNIFIED, made worthy, ennobled; 2. 3. 22

DIGNITY, worthiness, nobility, social position, Prol. 1

DIGRESS, depart, deviate; 3. 3. 127

DIRE, DIREFUL, dreadful, horrible; 5. 3. 225, 247

DISCOVER, reveal, 2. 2. 106; 3. 1. 141

DISCOVERY, exploration, investigation; 1. 1. 149

DISCREET circumspect, 'sanely discriminating' (K.); 1. 1. 192

DISHCLOUT, dishcloth (freq. used in contemptuous comparison); 3. 5. 219

DISLIKE, displease; 2. 2. 61

DISMAL, (i) gloomy, dreadful, 'striking the mind with dismay' (Schmidt; cf. O.E.D. 4); 3. 2. 44; (ii) dreadful, horrifying; 4. 3. 19

DISPLANT, uproot; 3. 3. 60

DISPOSITION(s), (i) inclination; 1. 3. 66; (ii) mental constitution or temperament; 3. 3. 115

DISPUTE OF, discuss; 3. 3. 64

DISTANCE (in fencing), 'a definite interval of space to be observed between two combatants' (O.E.D. 5 b); 2. 4. 21

DISTEMPERATURE, mental disturbance; 2. 3. 40

DISTEMPERED, disordered, distracted; 2. 3. 33

DISTILLED, extracted; 4. 1. 94; 5. 3. 15

DIVINE (sb.), ecclesiastic; 3. 3. 50

DIVISION, (a) 'execution of a rapid melodic passage' (O.E.D. 7); (b) separation; 3. 5. 29

DO GOOD (to someone), benefit, assist (esp. with money); 3. 5. 194

DOCTRINE, instruction, lesson; 1. 1. 237

Doom (sb.), (i) judgement, sentence; 3. 3. 4, 8, 9, 60; (ii) 'general doom' — Day of Judgement; 3. 2. 67

Doom (vb.), adjudge; 3. 1. 133

Doomsday, last day of life; 3. 3. 9; 5. 3. 234

Doting, violently in love; 3. 3. 68

Doubt (sb.), hesitation; 4. 1. 87

Doubt (vb.), suspect; 5. 3. 44

Down, (i) abed; 3. 5. 66; 4. 5. 12; (ii) brought low in death (with quibble on (i)); 5. 3. 209

Drawer, tapster; 3. 1. 9

Drift, (i) meaning; 2. 3. 55; (ii) intention, or perhaps scheme (O.E.D. 5); 4. 1. 114

Drivel, (a) slaver, (b) talk nonsense; 2. 4. 89

Drum, drummer; 1. 4. 114

Dry-beat, thrash severely (properly, beat with blows which bruise but do not draw blood); 3. 1. 78; 4. 5. 122

Ducat, silver Ital. coin worth about 3s. 6d.; 5. 1. 59

Dull, heavy; 1. 4. 21; 2. 1. 2

Dump, tune (properly, melancholy tune); 4. 5. 105, 107

Dumps, low spirits; 4. 5. 126

Dwell on, stand on, be punctilious for; 2. 2. 88

Earth, body; 1. 2. 15; 3. 2. 59; (quibble on 'the earth', 'clay'), 2. 1. 2; 3. 3. 120

Effect, fulfilment; 1. 5. 106

Ell, 45 inches; 2. 4. 83

Endart, shoot as if a dart; 1. 3. 99

Engross, gain exclusive possession; 5. 3. 115

Enpierce, pierce through; 1. 4. 19

Entertain, conceive (the idea of); 3. 1. 170

Envious, (i) malicious; 1. 1. 150; 3. 1. 167; 3. 2. 40; 3. 5. 7; (ii) jealous; 2. 2. 4, 7

Estate, situation, condition; 3. 3. 64

Ethiop, Ethiopian, with black skin; 1. 5. 46

Excuse, defer with excuses (cf. O.E.D. 3 b); 2. 5. 34

Exhale, draw forth (v. *meteor*); 3. 5. 13

Expire, bring to an end; 1. 4. 109

Extremes, terrible (utmost) difficulties; 4. 1. 62

Extremity, desperate condition; 1. 3. 103

Fair (adj.), (the freq. sense of 'beautiful' occurs *passim*); (i) bright, broad; 1. 1. 138 (O.E.D. 12 b); (ii) used conventionally in polite address; 1. 1. 206 ('fair coz'); 2. 2. 98; 2. 4. 106; (iii) (in 'fair mark') (a) beautiful, (b) plainly to be seen, obvious (cf. O.E.D. 17); 1. 1. 206; (iv) favourable; 1. 2. 19; (v) fine, excellent; 1. 2. 74; 3. 5. 180; (vi) peaceable, agreeable; 1. 5. 73; (vii) civil, courteous; 2. 1. 11; (viii) decent, clean; 1. 1. 220; 2. 1. 28; (ix) benign; 2. 3. 19

Fair (adv.), courteously; 3. 1. 152

FAIR (sb.), (i) beautiful woman; 1. 1. 235; 2 Prol. 3; (ii) (a) fair complexion, (b) (i); 1. 1. 230; (iii) beauty; 1. 3. 91

FAIRLY, completely; 2. 4. 45

FALL BACKWARD, sc. in embrace of husband; 1. 3. 43, 57

FANTASTICO, ridiculous person; 2. 4. 29

FANTASY, imagination; 1. 4. 98

FASHION-MONGER, one who studies and follows the latest fashions; 2. 4. 33

FAST, sound asleep; 4. 5. 1

FATAL, (i) fraught with evil destiny; Prol. 5; (ii) producing death, destruction; 3. 1. 142, 165; 5. 1. 65

FAULT, lack, want; 2. 4. 118

FAY, faith; 1. 5. 126

FEARFUL, (i) dreadful, terrible; 1 Prol. 9; 1. 4. 108; 2 Prol. 8; 4. 3. 32; (ii) timorous, apprehensive; 3. 3. 1; 3. 5. 3; 5. 2. 16

FEARFULLY, dreadfully, terribly; 5. 3. 133

FEELING, deeply felt; 3. 5. 74

FEE-SIMPLE, absolute possession (lit. estate in perpetual possession of owner and his descendants); 3. 1. 31, 33

FETTLE, make ready; 3. 5. 153

FIELD, place of combat; 3. 1. 57

FIELD-BED, (a) camp-bed, (b) resting-place on open ground; 2. 1. 40

FILM, 'fine thread or filament, as of gossamer, silk, etc.' (O.E.D.); 1. 4. 66

FIND (abs.), discover (game) in hunting (O.E.D. 9 b); 2. 4. 126

FISH, female flesh (lit. 'harlot'; cf. 'fishmonger', Ham. 2. 2. 174, n.); 1. 1. 30

FLASK, powder-horn, carried on the belt not far from the 'match' (a piece of slow-burning rope, used to ignite the powder in the lock of the match-lock musket); 3. 3. 132

FLATTERING, (adj. and adv.), pleasing, pleasingly (with idea of deception); 2. 2. 141; 5. 1. 1

FLECKED. (a) dappled with bright spots (O.E.D. 3); (b) flushed or blotchy (O.E.D. 2 cites Burton, Anat. Mel. 'red and fleet ...as if they had been at a Mayor's feast'); 2. 3. 3

FLEER, grin contemptuously; 1. 5. 57

FLESH (vb.), to get oneself in flesh = to grow plump (O.E.D. 3); 5. 1. 84

FLIRT-GILL, giddy or loose woman; ('Gill' short for Gillian); 2. 4. 148

FLOW, abound; 2. 4. 39

FOND, (i) unwisely affectionate; 2. 2. 98; (ii) foolish; 3. 3. 53; (iii) combining i and ii; 4. 5. 82

FOOL, (i) term of endearment; 1. 3. 32, 49; (ii) dupe; 3. 1. 135

FOOL'S PARADISE, state of happiness based on illusion; 2. 4. 159

FOOT IT, dance; 1. 5. 27

FOR. Unusual senses: (i) 'for

For (*cont.*):
you' = ready to join issue with you; 1. 1. 53; (ii) as concerns; 3. 1. 98

Forfeit, penalty; (here) loss of life; 1. 4. 111

Form, (i) formal manners, conventional etiquette; 2. 2. 88; (with quibble on 'form' = bench) 2. 4. 34; (ii) likeness; 5. 3. 246

Frank, generous, bountiful; 2. 2. 131

French slop or 'trunk hose', short loose hanging breeches; 2. 4. 44

Friend, (i) lover, paramour (cf. *Meas.* 1. 4. 29); 3. 5. 43, 77; (ii) kinsman; 3. 3. 151; 3. 5. 75

Gall, (i) bitter poison; 1. 1. 193; (ii) bitterness; 1. 5. 92

Gape (vb.), long. Commonly used with 'heir'; 2. Prol. 2

Gear, orig. = clothes, (hence) stuff, goings-on, etc.; 2. 4. 98; 5. 1. 60

General, universal; 3. 2. 67

Gentle, (i) used before proper name or title as complimentary term in polite address; 1. 2. 16; 1. 4. 13; 1. 5. 65; 2. 2. 93; 3. 1. 83; 4. 3. 1; 5. 3. 59; (ii) (*a*) mild, (*b*) tender; 1. 5. 94

Ghostly, spiritual; 2. 2. 188; 2. 3. 45; 2. 6. 21; 3. 3. 50

Give you the..., call you...; (cf. *Macb.* 1. 3. 119); 4. 5. 114, 115

Gleek, gibe; 'give someone the gleek' = mock him, make a jest at his expense; 4. 5. 113

Glooming, dark, dismal; 5. 3. 305

Go, 'go to' = come, come! (expressing 'disapprobation, remonstrance, protest, or derisive incredulity', O.E.D.); 1. 5. 77, 78, 82; 2. 4. 178

Go to the wall, 'give way, succumb in a conflict or struggle' (O.E.D. wall, 13); 1. 1. 14

God-den or Good-den, good evening, good afternoon; 1. 2. 57; 2. 4. 107; 3. 1. 37

God gi' god-den, Godigoden, God ye good-den, = God give you good evening; 1. 2. 58; 2. 4. 106; 3. 5. 172

God's bread! Oath = by the bread consecrated for Communion; 3. 5. 176

God save the mark. Prob. orig. a formula to avert an evil omen, hence used by way of apology when something horrible etc. has been mentioned (O.D.P.); 3. 2. 53

God ye goodmorrow, God give you good morning; 2. 4. 105

Golden, (i) fine, excellent; 1. 3. 93; (ii) happy, refreshing; 2. 3. 38

Good-den, see *God-den*

Good heart, (i) familiar or affectionate form of address; 1. 1. 183; (ii) oath, = 'by God's heart'; 2. 4. 167

Goodman, 'prefixed to names of persons under the rank of gentleman, esp. yeomen or farmers' (O.E.D. 3b), hence applied here ironically to a presumptuous young gentleman; 1. 5. 77.

GOOD MORROW, (a) good morning; 1. 1. 159; 2. 3. 31; 2. 4. 46; (b) good-bye; 2. 3. 34

GORE BLOOD, clotted blood; 3. 2. 56

GOSSAMERS, threads of spider-web; 2. 6. 18

GOSSIP, (i) familiar friend; 2. 1. 11; (ii) tattling woman crony; 3. 5. 171, 174

GOWN, dressing-gown; 1. 1. 73 S.D.

GRACE, (i) favour; 1. 3. 60; 2. 3. 86; (ii) beneficent virtue, efficacy; 2. 3. 15; (iii) divine grace; 2. 3. 28

GRAVE, (i) dignified; 1. 1. 92; (ii) (a) solemn, (b) in, or ready for, a grave; 3. 1. 97

GRAVITY, weighty speech, serious talking (used ironically); 3. 5. 174

GREAT CHAMBER. Corresponded to modern drawing-room; 1. 5. 13

GREEN, pale, sickly; 2. 2. 8

GREEN IN EARTH, freshly laid in the grave; 4. 3. 42

GREEN-SICKNESS (as adj.), afflicted with the green-sickness (v. note on 2. 2. 8), hence miserably pallid; 3. 5. 156

GRIEVANCE, (i) trouble, distress; 1. 1. 156; (ii) cause of complaint; 3. 1. 51

GRIPING, agonizing; 4. 5. 125

GROUND, (i) earth; 5. 3. 179; (ii) cause; 5. 3. 180

GRUDGE, ill-will; Prol. 3

GYVES, fetters; 2. 2. 179

HA, 'An inarticulate vowel-sound, expressing hesitation or interruption in speech' (O.E.D. 3); 3. 3. 12; 3. 4. 19

HAI (It. lit.=you have it), home-thrust in fencing; 2. 4. 26

HAIR, 'against the hair'= contrary to my inclination (with quibble on pubic hair); 2. 4. 93

HALL, 'a hall!'=cry to make room (for a dance or the like); 1. 5. 27

HAND, 'at my hand'=from me; 3. 3. 5

HAP, fortune; 3. 3. 171; 'dear hap'=good fortune; 2. 2. 189

HAPPY, opportune; 5. 3. 169; 'in happy time', phrase expressing pleasure at good fortune, here = 'à propos' (Schmidt, On.), or 'how opportune, fortunate!' (spoken with concealed irony); 3. 5. 111

HARE, (a) the animal, (b) prostitute; 2. 4. 127–132

HARLOTRY, good-for-nothing wench; 4. 2. 14

HASTY, quick-acting; 5. 1. 64

HAVE AT THEE (you), 'App. 1st pers. plural, but often singular in sense, announcing the speaker's intent to get at or attack' (O.E.D. have, 20); 1. 1. 71; 4. 5. 122; 5. 3. 70

HAVE IT, have been given a home-thrust (cf. HAI); 3. 1. 106

HEAD, source of a river; fig. (as here) origin; 5. 3. 218

HEARTLESS, spiritless, cowardly; 1. 1. 65

HEARTS, good fellows; 1. 5. 86, 88

HEAVINESS, sadness; 3. 4. 11; 3. 5. 108

HEAVY, (i) sad; 2. 2. 157; (in quibbling contrast to 'light') 1. 1. 136, 177; 1. 4. 12; (ii) grievous; 3. 3. 157; 4. 5. 18; (with quibble on heavy in weight) 1. 1. 185; 3. 3. 60; (iii) sluggish; 2. 5. 17

HELEN. In classical mythology the most beautiful woman of her time, wife of the Greek Menelaus, seduced and carried off to Troy by the Trojan Paris, whence arose the Graeco-Trojan War; 2. 4. 42

HERO. In classical mythology a beautiful priestess of the goddess Aphrodite at Sestos on the European side of the Hellespont; she was loved by Leander who belonged to Abydos on the opposite shore; he was wont to swim to her at night, guided by a torch held up by her; one stormy night he was drowned, and she threw herself into the water; 2. 4. 42

HIGH-LONE, 'quite alone, without support' (O.E.D.). Prov. expr. (Tilley, G 157); 1. 3. 37

HILDING, jade, baggage (O.E.D. 2 b); 2. 4. 42; 3. 5. 168

HIND, menial; 1. 1. 65

HIT (sb.), striking of target with arrow, hence fig. guess; 1. 1. 207

HIT (vb.), (i) strike; 3. 1. 167; (ii) (a) strike with arrow, (b) copulate with (v. mark); 1. 1. 207; 2. 1. 33; (iii) 'hit it' = strike target with arrow, hence fig. guess; 2. 3. 41; 2. 4. 55

HOAR (adj.), (a) mouldy, (b) grey- or white-haired with age (with quibble on 'whore'); 2. 4. 128, 129, 130, 132

HOAR (vb.), (a) become mouldy, (b) become grey- or white-haired (with quibble on 'whore'); 2. 4. 134

HOLIDAME. Corruption of 'halidom' = holiness, (hence) relics upon which oaths were sworn, (hence) the formula 'by my halidome' which by association with 'dame' became 'holidame', so that the phrase was popularly taken as 'by our Lady' (v. O.E.D.); 1. 3. 44

HOLP, helped, remedied; 1. 2. 48

HOMELY, simple, straightforward; 2. 3. 55

HONEST, (i) honourable; 1. 5. 124; 2. 5. 55, 60; 3. 2. 62; (ii) respectable, seemly; 2. 1. 28; (iii) worthy; 2. 5. 78; 4. 5. 97

HOOD (? sb.); v. note; 4. 4. 13

HOOD (vb.), blindfold a hawk; 3. 2. 14

HOODWINKED, blindfolded; 1. 4. 4

HOT, (i) eager; 2. 5. 62; (ii) quick-tempered; 3. 5. 175; (iii) violent, raging; 3. 1. 159

HOUSE (fig.), sheath; 5. 3. 203

HUMOROUS, (a) moist, damp,

(b) whimsical, capricious, moody; 2. 1. 31

HUMOUR, (i) inclination; 1. 1. 128, 140; (ii) caprice; 2. 1. 7; (iii) morbid fluid; 4. 1. 96

HUNT'S-UP. Orig. a song entitled 'The Hunt Is Up', used to awaken huntsmen; hence, an early morning song, esp. one for the newly married (cf. Cotgrave, 'Resveil'); 3. 5. 34

HURDLE, 'a kind of frame or sledge on which traitors used to be drawn through the streets to execution' (O.E.D. 1c); 3. 5. 155

IDLE (adj.), foolish, silly; 1. 4. 97

IDLE (vb.), move lazily or uselessly; 2. 6. 19

ILL-BESEEMING, (i) inappropriate; 1. 5. 74; (ii) ill-sorted; hence, monstrous; 3. 3. 113

ILL-DIVINING, prophesying evil; 3. 5. 54

IMAGINED, in thought, inner; 2. 6. 28

IMPORT (sb.), importance; 5. 2. 19

IMPORT (vb.), signify; 5. 1. 28

IMPORTUNE, interrogate urgently and persistently; 1. 1. 144

IN, under, liable to; 1. 2. 2

INDITE, intentional blunder for 'invite' —satirizing the unintentional blunder of the previous speaker (cf. 2 Hen. IV, 2. 1. 27); 2. 4. 124

INHERIT, receive, enjoy the possession of; 1. 2. 30

IRON WIT, dull or stupid wit; (cf. R. III. G.); 4. 5. 123

JACK, (i) lad, chap; 3. 1. 11; (ii) rude fellow, knave; 2. 4. 147; 4. 5. 143

JAUNCE (sb. and vb.), prance. Cf. R. II. 5. 5. 94, and D.D. 'jance' (Suss. dial.)=weary or tiring journey. K. quotes 'jaunce' from Seneca's Ten Tragedies; 2. 5. 26, 52

JEALOUS, suspicious; 5. 3. 33; 'jealous hood' (v. note); 4. 4. 13

JOINED-STOOL, 'stool made by a joiner, as distinguished from one of more clumsy workmanship' (O.E.D.); 1. 5. 6

JUST (adv.), exactly; 3. 2. 78; 3. 3. 86

JUSTLY, (a) exactly, (b) honourably; 3. 2. 78

KEEP, (a) inhabit, (b) guard (fig. from notice, observation); 3. 2. 74

KINDLY, aptly, exactly. (Cf. as adj. in 1 H. VI, 3. 1. 131); 2. 4. 55

KNAVE, (i) servant; 1. 5. 28; (ii) rogue; 2. 4. 148, 150, 156; 4. 5. 142

LABEL, lit. a supplementary note or codicil to a legal document (O.E.D. 2), hence (here), such a note cancelling 'another deed'; 4. 1. 57

LACE, 'mark as with (gold or silver) lace or embroidery; diversify with streaks of colour' (O.E.D. 6); 3. 5. 8

i) wife; 3. 3. 98; (ii) ... s Lady'=the Virgin ...; 2. 5. 61; (iii) 'By 'r Lady', oath=by the Virgin Mary; 1. 5. 34

LADY-BIRD, (a) term of endearment, 'sweetheart', (b) light o' love (cf. O.E.D. 2, quot. 1700, and *Dict. Slang*); 1. 3. 3

LAMB, term of endearment, 'pet'; 1. 3. 3; 4. 5. 2

LAMMAS EVE, 31 July (day before Lammas-tide); 1. 3. 18, 22

LANGUISH, sickness, suffering; 1. 2. 49

LANTHORN, (i) a lighthouse (O.E.D. 3); or windowed turret on the roof of a (college) hall (O.E.D. 4); 5. 3. 84; (ii) lantern; 5. 3. 120 S.D.

LARGE, (a) lengthy, (b) licentious, gross, (c) (indelicately) large in size; 2. 4. 94

LAURA, lady to whom Petrarch (q.v.) wrote his love-sonnets; 2. 4. 39

LAY, (a) prevent (spirit) from 'walking', cause (spirit) to disappear, (b) (indelicately) cause (erection) to subside; 2. 1. 26

LAY HAND ON HEART, ref. to 'gesture used in protesting the reality of the feeling expressed' (Deighton); 3. 5. 190

LEARN, teach; 1. 4. 93; 3. 2. 12; 4. 2. 17

LEAVE, 'give leave' = kindly leave (us/me) alone, undisturbed; 1. 3. 8; 2. 5. 25; 'by your leaves' = with your permission; 2. 6. 36

LENTEN PIE, properly pie containing no meat and thus suitable for consumption in Lent; here perhaps meat pie consumed bit by bit surreptitiously in Lent and therefore mouldy before it is all eaten; 2. 4. 127–8

LETTERS, plur. with sing. sense; 4. 1. 114, 124; 5. 1. 13, 31

LEVEL, 'aim, line of aim' (K.); 3. 3. 103

LIGHT, (i) active, nimble, swift; 2. 2. 66; (with quibble on opposite of 'heavy') 1. 4. 20; (ii) immodest; 2. 2. 99; (with quibble on opposite of dark) 2. 2. 105; (iii) trivial, worthless (with quibble on opposite of 'heavy'); 2. 6. 20

LIGHTLY, joyfully; 5. 1. 3

LIGHTNESS, (a) light weight, (b) levity, frivolity; 1. 1. 177

LIST, please, wish; 1. 1. 41

LIVING, property, estate; 4. 5. 40

LODGING, night's resting-place (O.E.D. 3); 3. 2. 2

LOLL, stick out (sc. (a) the tongue, (b) the 'bauble', q.v.); 2. 4. 90

LONG SWORD, old fashioned two-hand sword (cf. *Wives*, 2. 1. 203; *Sh. Engl.* ii. 394, with picture on p. 393); 1. 1. 74

LOST, beside oneself, (here) love-lorn; 1. 1. 196

LURE (vb.), falcony term; used of a falconer recalling a hawk from flight by holding up to its sight a 'lure', i.e. a kind of leather frame, decked with feathers and garnished with pieces of meat, which the falconer carried in his hand (v. *Shrew.* G.); 2. 2. 159

LUSTY, vigorous, lively, merry; 1. 2. 26; 1. 4. 113; 2. 4. 146

MAKE AGAINST, provide evidence against; 5. 3. 225

MAMMET, doll, puppet; 3. 5. 184

MANAGE (sb.), conduct, 'course, rise and progress' (K.); 3. 1. 142

MANAGE (vb.), handle, wield; 1. 1. 68

MANDRAKE, poisonous plant, with forked root which was thought to resemble the human form; the plant was believed to utter shrieks when pulled from the ground, which shrieks were fatal to the hearer or drove him mad; 4. 3. 47

MANNERLY, seemly, decent; 1. 5. 98

MARCHPANE, marzipan, kind of sweetmeat; 1. 5. 8

MARGENT, (lit.) margin, (hence) marginal note, interpretation (cf. *Ham.* G.); 1. 3. 87

MARK (sb.), (i) target (with indelicate· *double entendre*); 1. 1. 206; 2. 1. 33; (ii) 'God save the mark', phrase used by way of apology for mentioning something disagreeable, prob. orig. a formula to avert an evil omen (cf. O.E.D. 'mark', sb.¹, 18); 3. 2. 53

MARK (vb.), 'mark to', designate for; 1. 3. 60

MARRIED, harmoniously blended; 1. 3. 84

MARRY (interj.), to be sure, indeed (orig. name of Virgin Mary used as oath); 1. 1. 37 and *passim*

MARRY COME UP, An exp. of 'indignant or amused surprise or contempt = "hoitytoity"' (O.E.D.). Cf. Tilley, C 740; 2. 5. 62

MARTYR, afflict with grievous pain; 4. 5. 59

MASQUE (sb.), ball attended by masked visitors;·1. 4. 48; 1. 5. 34

MASQUE (vb.), attend ball or assembly wearing masks; 1. 5. 38

MASS, mild oath, 'by the Mass' (church service); 4. 4. 19

MASTERLESS, without its owner (cf. *F. Q.* 1, vii. 19, 'His silver shield, now idle, maisterlesse'); 5. 3. 142

MATCHED, (i) compared; 2 Prol. 4; (ii) married; 3. 5. 178

MAW, stomach, 5. 3. 45

MEAGRE, thin, starved; 5. 1. 40

MEAN, means, method. With quibble; 3. 3. 46

MEASURE (sb.), (i) dance; 1. 5. 50; (ii) (a) dance, (b) standard; 1. 4. 10

MEASURE (vb.), (i) estimate; 1. 1. 125; (ii) (a) estimate, (b) mete out, (c) dance; 1. 4. 10

MEAT, (i) food (not flesh); 3. 1. 22; see also *baked*

MEAT (*cont.*):
meats; (ii) food (flesh);
3. 1. 106; (iii) (*a*) food
(flesh), (*b*) flesh of whore,
and hence whore; 2. 4. 131

MEDICINE, the physician's art;
2. 3. 24

MEDLAR, a fruit 'with a
large cup-shaped "eye" between the persistent calyx-
lobes. It is eaten when
decayed to a soft pulpy
state' (O.E.D.); here (*a*)
with quibble on 'meddle' =
to have sexual intercourse
(O.E.D. 5), and (*b*) by allusion to its obscene syno-
nym (v. note); 2. 1. 34, 36

METEOR. Supposedly engen-
dered from vapours drawn up
by the sun and then ignited;
3. 5. 13

MEW (vb.), shut up (as hawks
were shut in their 'mews'
or cages); 3. 4. 11

MICKLE, great; 2. 3. 15

MIND, pay attention to, brood
over; 4. 1. 13

MINION, hussy; 3. 5. 151

MINISTER, provide; 4. 3. 25

MISADVENTURED, unfortunate;
Prol. 7

MISSHAPEN, ill-directed
(O.E.D., 4 < Johnson's
Dict. Cf. *Ham.* 5. 2. 10,
'shapes our ends'; *Lear*, 1.
1. 190, 'shape his course');
3. 3. 131

MISTA'EN, gone astray (v.
O.E.D. 'mistake' vb. 3);
5. 3. 203

MISTEMPERED, tempered for
an evil purpose (with quibble
on sense of 'bad-tempered,
angered'); 1. 1. 86

MODERN, ordinary, common-
place; 3. 2. 120

MONUMENT, burial vault; 3.
5. 201; 5. 1. 18; 5. 2. 23;
5. 3. head S.D., 127, 193,
274

MOOD, anger; 3. 1. 12

MOODY, angry; 3. 1. 12, 13

MOUSE-HUNT, pursuer of women by night (v. note); 4.
4. 11

MOVE, (i) make angry; 1. 1.
6, 87; 3. 1. 13; 4. 5. 95;
(ii) impel; 1. 1. 7, 10; 3. 1.
12; 4. 3. 4; (iii) (*a*) (i), (*b*)
(ii); 1. 1. 8, 11; (iv) cause,
call forth; 1. 3. 98; 3. 2.
120; (v) take the initiative;
1. 5. 105; (vi) make a pro-
position to; 3. 4. 2

MUCH, (i) approximately; 1.
3. 73; (ii) 'much in years' =
advanced in age; 3. 5. 46

MUFFLE, (i) blindfold; 1. 1.
170; (ii) cover up, conceal;
5. 3. 21

MUTINY, strife, discord; Prol.
3; 1. 5. 80

NATIVE, (i) original, where you
were produced; 3. 2. 102;
(ii) natural, normal; 4. 1. 97

NATURAL (adj.), kindly; 2. 3.
12

NATURAL (sb.), congenital
idiot; 2. 4. 89

NATURE, natural affection (v.
Ham. G.); 4. 5. 82

NAUGHT, wicked; 3. 2. 87

NAY (in asseveration), indeed;
1. 3. 30, 79; 3. 1. 15; (in
protest) now then; 2. 5. 28

NEAR, (*a*) near the bull's-eye,
(*b*) accurately; 1. 1. 204; see
also *come near*

NEEDLY, of necessity; 3. 2. 117

NEIGHBOUR, neighbouring; 2. 6. 27

NICE, trivial; 3. 1. 153; 5. 2. 18

NIÊSS, or 'nyas', a young hawk in the aerie (< Fr. niais = nestling, an innocent girl (v. note)); 2. 2. 167

NIGHTLY, at night; 4. 1. 81

NOTE (sb.), marginal comment (v. note); 1. 1. 234

NOTE (vb.), (a) furnish with notes, (b) find fault with (O.E.D. 7); 4. 5. 119

NUMBERS, verse; 2. 4. 39

O (as sb.), lament (v. also circle); 3. 3. 91

OCCUPY, (a) dwell upon, (b) have to do with sexually (cf. 2 Hen. IV. 2. 4. 143 and G.); 2. 4. 97

O'ERPERCH, fly over; 2. 2. 66

OFFICE, duty; 4. 5. 85; 5. 1. 23

OLD, (i) vague epithet implying familiarity; 1. 4. 60; (ii) inveterate, hardened (cf. O.E.D. 5; with quibble on 'aged'); 3. 3. 94

OMIT, miss, neglect; 3. 5. 49

ONCE, at any time, ever; 1. 3. 62; 'at once' = once for all (note by J. C. Maxwell in M.L.R. xlix, p. 464); 3. 2. 57

OPEN-ARSE, medlar (v. note); 2. 1. 38

OPPRESSION, (i) distress, affliction; 1. 1. 183; 5. 1. 70; (ii) pressure, burden; 1. 4. 24

ORISON, prayer; 4. 3. 3

ORNAMENTS, equipment, attire; 1. 1. 92; 4. 2. 34

OSIER, made of willow twigs; 2. 3. 7

OUT, (i) at an end, expired; 1. 4. 3; (ii) exclamation expressing reproach, indignation, or anger; 3. 5. 156; (with 'upon you') 2. 4. 110; (with 'on her') 3. 5. 168; (iii) exclamation of lament; 4. 5. 25

OUTRAGE, (i) disgraceful tumult; 3. 1. 86; (ii) passionate outcry; 5. 3. 216

OVERWHELMING, overhanging; 5. 1. 39

OWE, possess, 2. 2. 46

PAIN, penalty or suffering for offence or crime, legal or theol. (cf. O.E.D. 1, 2 b); 1. 5. 94

PAINS, trouble, labour; 2. 4. 176, 185

PALMER, 'pilgrim who had returned from the Holy Land, in sign of which he carried a palm-branch or palm-leaf; also, an itinerant monk who travelled from shrine to shrine, under a perpetual vow of poverty; often simply an equivalent of pilgrim' (O.E.D.), with quibble on the sense of one who clasps another's palm with his own; 1. 5. 100, 101

PARDON, to give one his congé (cf. Gent. 3. 2. 98); 3. 5. 187

PART (sb.), (i) side (in a quarrel); 1. 1. 113; 'on part and part' = some on one side, some on the other; 1. 1. 113; (ii) (plur.) abilities, endowments, personal qualities; 3. 3. 2;

PART (*cont.*):
3. 5. 181; (iii) share; 4. 5.
69, 70; 'had part in'=
shared; 4. 5. 67

PARTIES OF SUSPICION, persons
suspected (of crime); 5. 3.
222

PARTISAN, spear with broad
head (v. *Ham.* G.); 1. 1. 71
S.D.; 93

PASSADO, It. thrust in fencing,
with one foot forward;
2. 4. 25; 3. 1. 84

PASSAGE, course; Prol. 9

PASSION, 'passionate speech or
outburst' (O.E.D. 6d); 2. 2.
104

PASSING, pre-eminently; 1. 1.
233, 235

PASTRY, place where pastry is
made, 4. 4. 2

PEEVISH, perverse, obstinate;
4. 2. 14

PENCIL, paintbrush; 1. 2. 41

PENNYWORTHS, allowances
(here, of sleep); 4. 5. 4

PENSIVE, sorrowful; 4. 1.
39

PENTECOST, Whitsuntide; 1.
5. 37

PEPPER (vb.), 'give (one)
his death-blow, "do for"'
(O.E.D. 5b), make an end
of; 3. 1. 98

PETRARCH, 14th cent. Ital.
poet who wrote famous
love-sonnets; 2. 4. 39

PHAËTON, in Gk. mythology,
son of the sun-god Phoebus;
he begged, and was allowed,
to drive his father's sun-
chariot on one occasion, but
he drove it too near the earth,
and Zeus, chief of the gods,
slew him with a thunder-
bolt to save the world from
conflagration; 3. 2. 3

PILCHER. App. an extension of
'pilch'= an 'outer garment
of skin or leather', here fig.
(contemptuous) = scabbard
(O.E.D.); 3. 1. 79

PIN, stud in centre of the
archer's target; 2. 4. 15

PINK, acme, perfect example
(with quibble on (*a*) name
of flower and (*b*) 'pink'=
rapier-thrust); 2. 4. 57

PIPE, 'put up one's pipes'=
cease from action, speaking,
etc., desist, 'shut up'
(O.E.D. 1e); 4. 5. 96

PITCH, height (a falcon's
'pitch' is the height to which
it soars before swooping
down on its prey); 1. 4. 21

POISE, weigh; 1. 2. 98

POOR JOHN, salted and dried
hake, 'a type of poor fare'
(O.E.D.), applied fig. to
a person; 1. 1. 31

POPERIN PEAR, variety of pear
named from Poperinghe, a
town in West Flanders (with
an indelicate quibble); 2. 1. 38

PORTENTOUS, foreboding misfortune, of evil omen; 1. 1.
140

PORTLY, dignified; 1. 5. 66

POST, (i) 'take post'=start out
with 'post horses' (q.v.);
5. 1. 21; (ii) 'in post'=in
haste by means of post
horses 5. 3. 273

POST HORSES, horses for rapid
travel, available for hire at
post-houses or inns; a long
journey would involve the
use of post horses in re-
lays; 5. 1. 26

Pox, 'the pox of'—a plague on; 2. 4. 28

PRACTISE, contrive, plot; 3. 5. 209

PRATING, idly chattering; 2. 4. 193

PRESENCE, (i) aspect, demeanour; 1. 5. 73; (ii) presence-chamber, room of state; 5. 3. 86

PRESENT, immediate; 4. 1. 61; 5. 1. 51

PRESENTLY, immediately; 4. 1. 54; 5. 1. 21

PRETTY, not inconsiderable; 1. 3. 11

PREVAIL, avail, have effect; 3. 3. 61

PRICK (sb.), (a) point on clock face, (b) penis; 2. 4. 109

PRICK (vb.), (i) (a) torment, grieve (O.E.D. 2), (b) stimulate, excite (O.E.D. 10); 1. 4. 28; (ii) remove by pricking with needle; 1. 4. 69

PRICKING, (a) hurting, (b) copulation; 1. 4. 28

PRIDE, splendour; 1. 2. 10; (with quibble on 'pride'= sexual desire); 1. 3. 90

PRINCOX, saucy youngster; 1. 5. 86

PROCURE, (i) cause; 2. 2. 145; bring; 3. 5. 67

PRODIGIOUS, monstrous, deformed, ill-omened; 1. 5. 140

PROFANER, one who puts something to an unworthy use; 1. 1. 81

PROMISE, assure; 3. 4. 6

PROOF (sb.), (i) 'in proof'—by the test of experience; 1. 1. 169; (ii) proved or tested armour; 1. 1. 209

PROOF (adj.), invulnerable; 2. 2. 73

PROPAGATE, augment (cf. *Tim.* 1. 1. 67); 1. 1. 186

PROPER, handsome; 2. 4. 197

PROPORTION, rhythm; 2. 4. 21

PROPORTIONED, formed, shaped; 3. 5. 182

PROROGUE, postpone; 2. 2. 78; 4. 1. 48

PROUD, elated, gratified; 3. 5. 143

PROVERBED, supplied with a proverb; 1. 4. 37

PULING, whimpering; 3. 5. 183

PUMP, light shoe; 2. 4. 60, 62

PUNTO REVERSO, (Ital.) backhanded thrust in fencing (lit. sword-point reversed); 2. 4. 25–6

PURBLIND, quite blind (cf. *L.L.L.* 3. 1. 178); 2. 1. 12

PURCHASE OUT, buy off, buy immunity for; 3. 1. 192

PURGE, purify; 1. 1. 190

QUESTION, converse, talk; 5. 3. 158

QUIT; requite; 2. 4. 185

QUOTE, notice, observe; 1. 4. 31

RAGE, frenzy, madness; 4. 3. 53

REARWARD, rearguard; (fig.) 'with a rearward'=as a subsequent event (with poss. quibble on 'rearword'— v. note); 3. 2. 121

REASON OF, discuss; 3. 1. 51

REBECK, early kind of fiddle; used as personal name; 4. 5. 132

RECEPTACLE, sepulchre (cf. *Titus*, G.); 4. 3. 39

RECKONING, estimation, repute; 1. 2. 4; (with quibble on 'counting, enumeration'); 1. 2. 33

RECLAIM, reduce to obedience; 4. 2. 47

REEKY, 'that emits vapour; steamy; full of rank moisture' (O.E.D. 1a); 4. 1. 83

REFLEX, reflection; 3. 5. 20

RESIGN, submit oneself; 3. 2. 59

RESPECTIVE, 'discriminating, partial' (O.E.D. 2b), having respect to who a person is; 3. 1. 122

REST, (i) 'rest you merry'= God keep you happy; 1. 2. 63, 84; (ii) 'set up one's rest'= properly, in card game of primero, stake one's all; hence fig. be firmly determined; 4. 5. 6 (with quibble on 'rest'=stake); 5. 3. 110

RETORT (of a blow), return; 3. 1. 163

ROOD, cross on which Christ was crucified; 1. 3. 37

ROPERY, 'trickery, knavery' (O.E.D.), '(here) "rascally talk"' (K.); [Q1 'rope-ripe'=fit for the gallows]; 2. 4. 141

ROSEMARY. Used at both weddings and funerals as symbol of remembrance; ... 205; 4. 5. 79 ... nt, disorderly; ... 188; (ii) ... 5. 51; (iii) ... unrestrained;

2. 3. 28; (iv) churlish, boorish, barbarous; 3. 3. 24

RUNAGATE, vagabond; 3. 5. 89

RUSH ASIDE, force out of place (O.E.D. v²); 3. 3. 26

SADLY, seriously; 1. 1. 200

SADNESS, seriousness, earnest (with quibble on 'sorrow'); 1. 1. 198, 201, 203

SAINT, adored one, mistress (cf. p. xx, Introd. *1 H. VI*); 1. 1. 213; 1. 5. 101; 2. 2. 55

SAUCY, insolent, impudent. A stronger term than in the mod. sense; 1. 5. 83; 2. 4. 140

SAVE-YOUR-REVERENCE. Orig. an apology for introducing an offensive word or expr. Here a sb. used attributively= human dung (cf. O.E.D. 'sir-reverence', 2); 1. 4. 42

SCANT, scarcely; 1. 2. 102

SCAPE, escape; 3. 1. 3; 4. 1. 75

SCATHE, injure; 1. 5. 84

SCOPE, area, 'field'; 1. 2. 18

SEARCHER, 'a person appointed to view dead bodies and to make report upon the cause of death' (O.E.D. 2 e); 5. 2. 8

SEASON (vb.), (a) preserve (by salting), (b) give a flavour, relish, zest, to; 2. 3. 72

SECRET, reticent, secretive; 2. 4. 184

SENTENCE, pithy saying, maxim; 2. 3. 79

SENTENTIOUS, speaker's blunder for 'sentences' or 'sententias' (=Lat. *sententiae*), pointed, witty sayings; 2. 4. 204

SERVE GOD (v. note); 2. 5. 45

SET, (i) stationed, posted; 3. 3. 148, 167; (ii) valued; 5. 3. 301

SETTLED (of the blood), congealed or 'ceased to flow' (O.E.D. 'settle' 22b), or 'flown back to the heart' (cf. *R. III*, 1. 2. 59, n.; *Caes.* 2. 1. 289, n.); 4. 5. 26

SHAKE, (*a*) quake, (*b*) bestir oneself (v. O.E.D. 6 g); 1. 3. 34

SHANK, shin-bone; 4. 1. 83

SHARP (adj.), (i) pungent in taste; 2. 4. 80; (ii) hungry; 5. 1. 41

SHARP (sb.), shrill high note; 3. 5. 28

SHIELD, 'God shield'=God forbid; 4. 1. 41

SHRIFT, (i) confession; 1. 1. 158; 2. 4. 174; 2. 5. 66; 4. 2. 15; (ii) absolution; 2. 3. 56

SHRIVE, give absolution after confession; 2. 4. 176

SIEGE, fig. assault; 1. 1. 211; 5. 3. 237

SIMPLE (adj.), (i) foolish; 2. 5. 38; 3. 1. 33; (ii) plain, mere; 3. 2. 16

SIMPLE (sb.), medicinal herb (called 'simple' because used in the production of medicinal 'compounds'); 5. 1. 40

SIMPLENESS, foolishness; 3. 3. 78

SINGLENESS, (*a*) fact of being one, (*b*) simplicity, silliness (cf. *2 H. IV*, 1. 2. 180); 2. 4. 66

SINGLE-SOLED, (*a*) (of footwear) 'having a single thickness of material in the sole' (O.E.D.), (*b*) (fig., of persons, here of a jest) 'poor, mean, of little account or worth' (O.E.D.); 2. 4. 65

SINGULAR, unmatched, unique; 2. 4. 64, 65

SKAINS-MATES. Meaning uncertain; various conjectures, e.g. 'cut-throat companions' (Malone), 'sempstresses, a word not always used in the most honourable acceptation' (Douce), etc.; 2. 4. 149

SLIP, (*a*) counterfeit coin, (*b*) evasion; 2. 4. 48

SLOP, v. *French slop*; 2. 4. 44

SLUG-A-BED, one slow to arise (cf. *R. III*, G. 'slug'); 4. 5. 2

SMALL, thin, fine; 1. 4. 64

SMATTER, chatter; 3. 5. 171

SOFT (interj.), stay!, stop!, wait a minute!; 1. 1. 194; 2. 2. 2; 3. 4. 18; 3. 5. 141

SOLACE IN, be happy in; 4. 5. 47

SOLELY, absolutely; 2. 4. 63, 65

SOLEMN, pertaining to a ceremony (here the marriage ceremony), hence 'festive, joyful'; 4. 5. 88

SOLEMNITY, 'occasion of ceremony; observance or celebration of special importance' (O.E.D.); (i) ref. to Capulet's ball; 1. 5. 57, 63; (ii) ref. to the (projected) nuptials of Juliet and Paris; 4. 5. 61

SOON-SPEEDING, *either* of quick effect *or* rapidly fatal; 5. 1. 60

SORT, choose, select; 4. 2. 34; 'sort out', choose, select, contrive; 3. 5. 109

Sound, (i) (a) utter, express, (b) measure the depth of; 3. 2. 126; (ii) make music; 4. 5. 134

Sounding, (i) measuring of depth, investigation (by others of his innermost feelings); 1. 1. 149; (ii) making music; 4. 5. 139

Soundly, thoroughly; 3. 1. 107; (with quibble on 'in musical sounds'); 4. 5. 111

Soundpost, 'small peg of wood fixed beneath the bridge of a violin or similar instrument, serving as a support for the belly and as a connecting part between this and the back' (O.E.D.); as a personal name; 4. 5. 135

Sparing, (a) refraining, (b) thrift; 1. 1. 217

Sped, dispatched, done for; 3. 1. 90

Speed, 'be my speed'=be my assistance, prosper me; 5. 3. 121

Spent, (i) (a) consumed, (b) worn out; 2. 4. 128, 134; (ii) shed; 3. 2. 130

Spinner, spider; 1. 4. 62

Spite (sb.), (i) contemptuous defiance; 1. 1. 77; 1. 5. 62; (ii) vexation; 2. 1. 27; (iii) injury; 4. 1. 31

Spite (vb.), injure; 4. 5. 55

Spleen, fiery temper, impetuosity; 3. 1. 156

Stair, ladder; 2. 4. 182

Stand, (i) (a) make a stand, fight, (b) stand still; 1. 1. 10, 11; (ii) (a) hold one's own, (b) stand in a row; 1. 2. 33; (iii) stand upright (with indelicate quibble); 1. 1. 28; 2. 1. 25; (iv) 'stand on'=attach importance to, insist on; 2. 3. 93; 2. 4. 33–4; (v) 'stand to'=maintain; 2. 4. 144; (vi) 'here stands'=herein consists; 3. 3. 166; (vii) 'stand aloof'=keep away, withdraw to a distance (cf. *Merch.* 3. 2. 42; O.E.D. 3); 5. 3. 1, 26

Star-crossed, thwarted by adverse influence of the stars; Prol. 6

State, (i) pomp, splendid array; 1. 4. 70; (ii) high rank; 3. 3. 34; (iii) fortunes; 3. 3. 166; (iv) condition; 4. 3. 4; (v) ceremony; 4. 3. 8

Stay, (i) undergo (cf. *Caes.* 5. 1. 106); 1. 1. 211; (ii) wait, await; 2. 5. 36; 4. 5. 144; (with 'on') 1. 2. 37; (iii) stop; 2. 3. 26; 4. 3. 57; 5. 3. 187, 251

Stead, help, benefit; 2. 3. 54

Still, ever, always; 1. 1. 170, and *passim*

Still-waking, always awake; 1. 1. 180

Stint, cease; 1. 3. 49, 58, 59

Stone, testicle; 1. 3. 54

Store, property, capital; 1. 1. 215

Stout, brave, valiant; 3. 1. 168, 172

Straight, straightway; 1. 3. 104, and *passim*

Strain, (i) force; 2. 3. 19; (ii) 'strain courtesy'='act with less than due courtesy' (On.); 2. 4. 50; (iii) utter in song (O.E.D. 22b); 3. 5.

28; (iv) tax one's resources;
4. 1. 47

STRANGE, (i) distant, reserved;
2. 2. 101, 102; (ii) (a) shy,
(b) unfamiliar; 3. 2. 15

STRATAGEM, deed of violence;
3. 5. 209

STREAM, emit beams of light;
2. 2. 21

STUFFED (WITH), (a) full (of)
(cf. *Ado.*, 1. 1. 53); (b) with
an indelicate reference (cf.
Ado, G. on 'a maid and
stuffed'); 3. 5. 181

SUBTLY, craftily, treacher-
ously; 4. 3. 25

SUDDEN, (i) immediate; 2. 3.
93; 3. 5. 136; (ii) quickly
effective; 3. 3. 46; (iii) soon
to come; 3. 5. 109

SULLEN, mournful; 4. 5. 88

SUPPLE GOVERNMENT = power
of motion; 4. 1. 102

SURCEASE, cease; 4. 1. 97

SWEET, (a) savoury, (b) dear
(cf. '*sweet* fellow'); 2. 4. 81

SWEET WATER, perfumed water;
5. 3. 14

SWEETING, sweet kind of
apple; 2. 4. 79

SWITCH AND SPURS! To ride
'switch and spur' = to gallop
at full speed (O.E.D. 'spur',
2a). Cf. Tilley, S 1046; 2.
4. 69

SWOUND, swoon; 3. 2. 56

SYMPATHY, agreement in feeling; 3. 3. 86

TACKLED, made of rope; 2. 4.
182

TAKE DOWN, *either* humiliate,
abate the arrogance of, *or*
rebuke (v. O.E.D. take,
80c); 2. 4. 145–6

TAKE ME WITH YOU, be explicit
so that I can follow your
meaning (cf. *1 H. IV*, 2. 4.
451); 3. 5. 141

TAKE THE WALL, keep, as one
walks, beside the wall, this
being the safest and cleanest
part of the street, since the
gutter was in the middle
(cf. O.E.D. 'wall', 16); hence,
fig., 'take the wall of someone' = get the better of him
(as if forcing him to walk
on a portion of street less
safe and clean). London
streets were very narrow
and without side-pave-
ments; 1. 1. 12

TALE, story (with quibble on
'tail' = penis); 2. 4. 92, 94,
96

TALL, valiant; 2. 4. 30

TALLOW-FACE, pale wretch; 3.
5. 157

TARTAR'S BOW, (v. note); 1. 4.
5

TASSEL-GENTLE or tercel-
gentle, male peregrine falcon; 2. 2. 159

TEAR, burst; 2. 2. 161

TEEN, sorrow; 1. 3. 14

TEMPER (sb.), (a) disposition,
(b) the quality of steel;
3. 1. 114

TEMPER (vb.), (i) modify;
2 Prol. 14; (ii) mix, com-
pound; 3. 3. 115; (iii) (a)
(ii), (b) (i); 3. 5. 97

TENDER (sb.), offer (of love or
marriage); 3. 4. 12; 3. 5.
184

TENDER (vb.), value, have re-
gard for; 3. 1. 70

TETCHY, fretful, peevish; 1. 3.
33

TEXT, 'a certain text'—a very true quoted saying; 4. 1. 21

THINK LONG, yearn, be impatient for (v. O.E.D. 'think', vb.², 10c); 4. 5. 41

THISBE, in classical mythology, a maiden beloved by Pyramus, a youth of Babylon. (Their story, told in Ovid, *Met.* bk. iv, bears certain resemblances to that of Romeo and Juliet; and forms the subject of the mechanicals' play in *M.N.D.*); 2. 4. 42

TILT, thrust; 3. 1. 157

TIME, 'in good time'= at the right moment, well met; 1. 2. 44–5.

TIMELESS, untimely; 5. 3. 162

TITAN, classical sun-god who travels through the sky in his chariot; 2. 3. 4

TITHE-PIG, pig paid as tithe; 1. 4. 79

To, in comparison with; 2. 4. 39; 3. 5. 219

TONIGHT, last night; 1. 4. 50; 2. 4. 2

TOOL, (*a*) weapon, (*b*) penis; 1. 1. 31

TOPGALLANT. 'Top'= platform near the head of a mast (O.E.D. 'top' 9); 'top mast'= the second section of a mast above the deck; 'top gallant mast'= a mast above that; 'top gallant'= the platform for this top mast; 2. 4. 183

TOWARDS, in preparation, about to take place; 1. 5. 122

TOY, whim, fancy; 4. 1. 119

TRAFFIC, business, occupation; Prol. 12

TRANSPARENT, (*a*) (lit.) clear, (*b*) (fig.) manifest; 1. 2. 94

TRICK, capricious piece of behaviour; 1. 5. 84

TRIUMPH, exultation, 'rapturous delight' (O.E.D. 5); 2. 6. 10

TRIUMPHANT, magnificent, glorious; 5. 3. 83

TROW, 'I trow'=(i) I'm sure; 1. 3. 34; (ii) a surprised or indignant expletive; 2. 5. 62

TRUCKLE-BED, 'low bed running on truckles or castors, usually pushed beneath a high or "standing" bed when not in use' (O.E.D.); 2. 1. 39

TRUDGE, 'undignified equivalent of "walk"' (O.E.D. 1); 1. 2. 34; 1. 3. 35

TRUST, trustworthiness; 3. 2. 85

TRUTH, honesty (cf. *Lucr.* 1532, *Son.* 48. 14, etc.); 5. 1. 1

TRY, (i) find out by testing; 4. 2. 3; (ii) test; 4. 2. 5; (iii) prove by experience; 4. 3. 29

TWAIN, separated; 3. 5. 240

TYRANNOUS, cruel, pitiless; 1. 1. 169

TYRANT, cruel, pitiless person; 1. 1. 21; 3. 2. 75

UMPIRE. Legal term='a third person called upon to decide a matter submitted to arbitrators [here, 'my extremes and me'] who cannot agree'; 4. 1. 63

UNACCUSTOMED, not customary, strange; 3. 5. 90

UNADVISED, unconsidered; 2.
2. 118

UNATTAINTED, not infected
(cf. 1. 2. 50); 1. 2. 88

UNBOUND, (a) without a
binding, (b) unmarried; 1.
3. 88

UNBRUISED, unbattered; 2. 3.
37

UNCOMFORTABLE, 'causing
or involving discomfort'
(O.E.D. 1), bringing sorrow,
'cheerless' (Schmidt); 4. 5.
60

UNEVEN, not smooth, (fig.) full
of difficulties; 4. 1. 5

UNFURNISHED, unprovided; 4.
2. 10

UNMANNED, (term in falcon-
ry), unused to the presence
of a man, 'not trained or
broken in' (O.E.D. 3), with
quibble on sense of 'husband-
less'; 3. 2. 14

UNSTUFFED, 'not clogged with
cares' (K.); 2. 3. 37

UNTHRIFTY, unfortunate, un-
toward,   not   bringing
'thrift' (=success); 5. 3.
136

UP, (i) aroused, up in arms; 3.
1. 132; (ii) come along!; 3.
1. 138; (iii) completely;
4. 2. 41, 45; (iv) afoot (with
quibble on 'out of bed');
5. 3. 188; (v) 'up and down'
=hither and thither, all
over the place; 2. 4. 90;
2. 5. 52

URGE, (i) mention, speak,
speak of; 1. 1. 202; 1. 5.
109; 3. 1. 153; (ii) provoke;
5. 3. 63

USE, (i) be accustomed; 2
Prol. 10; 3. 5. 189; (ii)

treat; 2. 4. 150; (iii) have
sexual   intercourse   with
(O.E.D. 10 b); cf. Per. 4. 6.
150, 'use her at thy
pleasure'; 2. 4. 151

UTTER, put on the market, sell;
5. 1. 67

VAIN, empty, foolish; 1. 4. 98

VALIDITY, value, worth; 3. 3.
33

VANITY, (i) frivolity; 1. 1. 177;
(ii) the delights of this world;
2. 6. 20

VAST, (a) extensive; (b) de-
solate; 2. 2. 83

VAULTY, arched; 3. 5. 22

VERSAL, 'Illiterate or colloq.
abbrev. of "universal"'
(O.E.D.); 2. 4. 199

VESTAL, chaste; 2. 2. 8; 3. 3.
38

VEX, (i) agitate; 1. 1. 191;
(ii) annoy; 2. 4. 155; (iii)
distress; 3. 5. 95

VIEW, (i) appearance; 1. 1.
168; (ii) eyesight; 1. 1. 170

VILE, (i) worthless; 1. 4. 111;
2. 3. 17; 3. 2. 59; (ii) evil,
base, filthy; 3. 1. 72, 140;
3. 2. 83; 3. 3. 106; 5. 3. 54

VILLAIN, term of address to a
servant, without implication
of bad qualities; 3. 1. 93

VIRTUE, beneficial power,
medicinal quality; 2. 3. 13

VISOR, (i) mask; 1. 4. 30;
1. 5. 23; (ii) face; 1. 4. 30

VOICE, vote; 1. 2. 19

WALK, step aside, come with
me in private; 3. 1. 74

WANNY, pallid; 4. 1. 100

WANT, WANT OF, lack; 2. 2.
78, 155; 5. 3. 15

WANTON (adj.), (i) *either* 'luxuriant' (Schmidt) *or* 'ungoverned, uncontrolled' (K.); 2. 5. 70; (ii) sportive, frolicsome; 2. 6. 19

WANTON (sb.), (i) trifler, unrestrained merrymaker; 1. 4. 35; (ii) spoiled or playful child; 2. 2. 177

WARRANT, assert as true, declare; 1. 3. 47, 53; 2. 5. 56; 3. 1. 98; 4. 5. 5; with 'him' or 'her',='concerning him or her'; 2. 5. 44; 4. 5. 1; with 'you',='to you'; 2. 4. 197; 4. 2. 40

WASHING, swashing, 'slashing with great force' (O.E.D. cf. Jonson, *Staple*, 5. 5. 15); 1. 1. 62

WASTE, expend, use up; 1. 4. 45

WATCH (sb.), watchmen, night-police; 3. 3. 148, 167; 5. 3. 71, 158, 279, 285

WATCH (vb.), (i) watch for the moment of; 4. 1. 116; (ii) stay awake; 4. 4. 8, 9, 12; (iii) prevent by vigilance; 4. 4. 12

WATERY, *either* 'controlling the tides' (On.), *or* 'pale' (O.E.D. 3); 1. 4. 65

WAX, (i) 'a man of wax'=a man perfect in beauty, like a wax model (O.E.D. 3c, doubtfully); 1. 3. 77; (ii) 'a form of wax'=a wax figure, lacking in essential human attributes; 3. 3. 126

WAYS, 'go thy ways'=go on your way (adverbial genitive sing.); 2. 5. 44

WEAK, 'stupid' (Schmidt), unworthy of a gentleman' (K.), but *v. n.*; 2. 4. 163

WEEDS, clothes; 5. 1. 39

WERADAY, alas. A variant of 'well-a-day'; 3. 2. 37; 4. 5. 15

WHAT, how; 1. 5. 55

WHORESON, coarse term of abuse, but sometimes (as here) of jocular familiarity; fellow, 'dog'; 4. 4. 19

WILD-GOOSE CHASE, 'a kind of horse-race or sport in which the second or any succeeding horse had to follow accurately the course of the leader (at a definite interval), like a flight of wild geese' (O.E.D.); here fig., and with a suggestion of 'flighty, foolish, fantastic person' in 'wild-goose'; 2. 4. 71

WILFUL, willing, eager; 1. 5. 89

WINDOW, shutter (v. *Caes*. G.); 1. 1. 138; "eyes' windows"=eyelids; 4. 1. 100

WINK, lit. shut, shut the eyes; hence, wink at, connive at (O.E.D., 5, 6.); 3. 2. 6; 5. 3. 294

WIT, (i) wisdom, prudence; 1. 1. 208; 1. 4. 49; (ii) wisdom, understanding, intelligence; 1. 3. 43; 3. 3. 122, 125, 130; 3. 5. 73; (iii) (plur.) mental faculties; 2. 4. 67, 71, 73; 4. 1. 47; (iv) wittiness, power of witty invention, 'mental quickness or sharpness' (O.E.D. 5); 2. 4. 79, 82; 4. 5. 121, 122, 123; (v) 'five wits'='usually, the five (bodily) senses; often vaguely, the perceptions or mental faculties generally'

(O.E.D. 'wit', 3b); 1. 4. 47;
cf. also 2. 4. 71–3

WITHAL, (i) thereby; 1. 1.
111; (ii) with; 1. 5. 115,
143; 3. 1. 77; (iii) in ad-
dition; 3. 1. 153

WOES, (i) pitiful objects; 5. 3.
179; (ii) sorrows; 5. 3. 180

WOMB, belly; 5. 3. 45

WORD, motto; 1. 4. 40

WORSHIPPED, venerated; 1. 1.
117

WOT, know; 3. 2. 139

WREAK, avenge; 3. 5. 101

WRETCH, term of endearment;
1. 3. 45

WROUGHT, prevailed upon
(O.E.D. 'work', 14); 3. 5.
144

ZOUNDS, an oath, short for
'God's wounds', i.e. the
wounds of Christ on the
cross; 3. 1. 48, 99

WORDSWORTH CLASSICS

General Editors: Marcus Clapham & Clive Reynard

JANE AUSTEN
Emma
Mansfield Park
Northanger Abbey
Persuasion
Pride and Prejudice
Sense and Sensibility

ARNOLD BENNETT
Anna of the Five Towns
The Old Wives' Tale

R. D. BLACKMORE
Lorna Doone

M. E. BRADDON
Lady Audley's Secret

ANNE BRONTË
Agnes Grey
The Tenant of Wildfell Hall

CHARLOTTE BRONTË
Jane Eyre
The Professor
Shirley
Villette

EMILY BRONTË
Wuthering Heights

JOHN BUCHAN
Greenmantle
The Island of Sheep
John Macnab
Mr Standfast
The Thirty-Nine Steps
The Three Hostages

SAMUEL BUTLER
Erewhon
The Way of All Flesh

LEWIS CARROLL
Alice in Wonderland

M. CERVANTES
Don Quixote

ANTON CHEKHOV
Selected Stories

G. K. CHESTERTON
The Club of QueerTrades
Father Brown: Selected Stories
The Man Who Was Thursday
The Napoleon of Notting Hill

ERSKINE CHILDERS
The Riddle of the Sands

**SELECTED BY
REX COLLINGS**
*Classic Victorian and
Edwardian Ghost Stories*

WILKIE COLLINS
The Moonstone
The Woman in White

JOSEPH CONRAD
Almayer's Folly
Heart of Darkness
Lord Jim

Nostromo
Sea Stories
The Secret Agent
Selected Short Stories
Victory

J. FENIMORE COOPER
The Last of the Mohicans

STEPHEN CRANE
The Red Badge of Courage

**EDITED BY
DAVID STUART DAVIES**
Shadows of Sherlock Holmes

THOMAS DE QUINCEY
*Confessions of an English
Opium Eater*

DANIEL DEFOE
Moll Flanders
Robinson Crusoe

CHARLES DICKENS
Barnaby Rudge
Bleak House
Christmas Books
David Copperfield
Dombey and Son
Ghost Stories
Great Expectations
Hard Times
Little Dorrit
Martin Chuzzlewit
*The Mystery of
Edwin Drood*
Nicholas Nickleby
Old Curiosity Shop
Oliver Twist
Our Mutual Friend
Pickwick Papers
A Tale of Two Cities

BENJAMIN DISRAELI
Sybil

FYODOR DOSTOEVSKY
Crime and Punishment
The Idiot

SIR ARTHUR CONAN DOYLE
*The Adventures of Sherlock
Holmes*
*The Case-Book of Sherlock
Holmes*
The Return of Sherlock Holmes
The Lost World & Other Stories
Sir Nigel
The White Company

**EDITED BY
DAVID STUART DAVIES**
The Best of Sherlock Holmes

GEORGE DU MAURIER
Trilby

ALEXANDRE DUMAS
The Count of Monte Cristo
The Three Musketeers

MARIA EDGEWORTH
Castle Rackrent

GEORGE ELIOT
Adam Bede
Daniel Deronda
Felix Holt the Radical
Middlemarch
The Mill on the Floss
Silas Marner

HENRY FIELDING
Tom Jones

RONALD FIRBANK
Valmouth & Other Stories

F. SCOTT FITZGERALD
*The Diamond as Big as the Ritz
& Other Stories*
The Great Gatsby
Tender is the Night

GUSTAVE FLAUBERT
Madame Bovary

JOHN GALSWORTHY
In Chancery
The Man of Property
To Let

ELIZABETH GASKELL
Cranford
North and South

GEORGE GISSING
New Grub Street

OLIVER GOLDSMITH
The Vicar of Wakefield

KENNETH GRAHAME
The Wind in the Willows

**GEORGE & WEEDON
GROSSMITH**
Diary of a Nobody

H. RIDER HAGGARD
She

THOMAS HARDY
*Far from the
Madding Crowd*
Jude the Obscure
The Mayor of Casterbridge
A Pair of Blue Eyes
The Return of the Native
Selected Short Stories
Tess of the D'Urbervilles
The Trumpet Major
Under the Greenwood Tree
Wessex Tales
The Woodlanders

NATHANIEL HAWTHORNE
The Scarlet Letter

O. HENRY
Selected Stories

JAMES HOGG
*The Private Memoirs and
Confessions of a Justified Sinner*

HOMER
The Iliad
The Odyssey

E. W. HORNUNG
Raffles: The Amateur
Cracksman

VICTOR HUGO
The Hunchback of
Notre Dame
Les Misérables
IN TWO VOLUMES

HENRY JAMES
The Ambassadors
Daisy Miller & Other Stories
The Europeans
The Golden Bowl
The Portrait of a Lady
The Turn of the Screw &
The Aspern Papers

M. R. JAMES
Ghost Stories

JEROME K. JEROME
Three Men in a Boat

JAMES JOYCE
Dubliners
A Portrait of the Artist as a
Young Man

TRANSLATED BY
EDWARD FITZGERALD
The Rubaiyat of
Omar Khayyam

RUDYARD KIPLING
The Best Short Stories
Captains Courageous
Kim
The Man Who
Would Be King
& Other Stories
Plain Tales from the Hills

D. H. LAWRENCE
The Plumed Serpent
The Rainbow
Sons and Lovers
Women in Love

SHERIDAN LE FANU
(EDITED BY M. R. JAMES)
In a Glass Darkly
Madam Crowl's Ghost
& Other Stories

GASTON LEROUX
The Phantom of the Opera

JACK LONDON
Call of the Wild & White Fang

KATHERINE MANSFIELD
Bliss & Other Stories

GUY DE MAUPASSANT
The Best Short Stories

HERMAN MELVILLE
Billy Budd & Other Stories
Moby Dick
Typee

GEORGE MEREDITH
The Egoist

H. H. MUNRO
The Collected Stories of Saki

THOMAS LOVE PEACOCK
Headlong Hall & Nightmare
Abbey

EDGAR ALLAN POE
Tales of Mystery and
Imagination

FREDERICK ROLFE
Hadrian the VII

SIR WALTER SCOTT
Ivanhoe
Rob Roy

WILLIAM SHAKESPEARE
All's Well that Ends Well
Antony and Cleopatra
As You Like It
The Comedy of Errors
Coriolanus
Hamlet
Henry IV Part 1
Henry IV Part 2
Henry V
Julius Caesar
King John
King Lear
Love's Labours Lost
Macbeth
Measure for Measure
The Merchant of Venice
The Merry Wives of Windsor
A Midsummer Night's Dream
Much Ado About Nothing
Othello
Pericles
Richard II
Richard III
Romeo and Juliet
The Taming of the Shrew
The Tempest
Titus Andronicus
Troilus and Cressida
Twelfth Night
Two Gentlemen of Verona
A Winter's Tale

MARY SHELLEY
Frankenstein

TOBIAS SMOLLETT
Humphry Clinker

LAURENCE STERNE
A Sentimental Journey
Tristram Shandy

ROBERT LOUIS STEVENSON
Dr Jekyll and Mr Hyde
The Master of Ballantrae
& Weir of Hermiston

BRAM STOKER
Dracula

R. S. SURTEES
Mr Sponge's Sporting Tour

JONATHAN SWIFT
Gulliver's Travels

W. M. THACKERAY
Vanity Fair

LEO TOLSTOY
Anna Karenina
War and Peace

ANTHONY TROLLOPE
Barchester Towers
Can You Forgive Her?
Dr Thorne
The Eustace Diamonds
Framley Parsonage
The Last Chronicle of Barset
Phineas Finn
The Small House at Allington
The Warden
The Way We Live Now

IVAN SERGEYEVICH
TURGENEV
Fathers and Sons

MARK TWAIN
Tom Sawyer &
Huckleberry Finn

JULES VERNE
Around the World in Eighty
Days & Five Weeks
in a Balloon
Journey to the Centre
of the Earth
Twenty Thousand Leagues
Under the Sea

VIRGIL
The Aeneid

VOLTAIRE
Candide

LEW WALLACE
Ben Hur

ISAAC WALTON
The Compleat Angler

EDITH WHARTON
The Age of Innocence

GILBERT WHITE
The Natural History
of Selborne

OSCAR WILDE
Lord Arthur Savile's Crime
& Other Stories
The Picture of Dorian Gray
The Plays
IN TWO VOLUMES

VIRGINIA WOOLF
Mrs Dalloway
Orlando
To the Lighthouse

P. C. WREN
Beau Geste

CHARLOTTE M. YONGE
The Heir of Redclyffe

TRANSLATED BY VRINDA
NABAR & SHANTA TUMKUR
Bhagavadgita

EDITED BY
CHRISTINE BAKER
The Book of Classic Horror
Stories

DISTRIBUTION

AUSTRALIA and PAPUA NEW GUINEA

Peribo Pty Ltd
58 Beaumont Road, Mount Kuring-Gai,
NSW 2080, Australia
Tel: (02) 457 0011 Fax: (02) 457 0022

CZECH REPUBLIC

Bohemian Ventures sro
Delnicka 13, 170 00 Prague 7
Tel: 042 2 877837 Fax: 042 2 801498

FRANCE

Copernicus Diffusion
81 Rue des Entrepreneurs, Paris 75015
Tel: 01 53 95 38 00 Fax: 01 53 95 38 01

GERMANY and AUSTRIA

Taschenbuch-Vertrieb Ingeborg Blank GmbH
Lager und Buro Rohrmooser Str 1,
85256 Vierkirchen/Pasenbach
Tel: 08139-8130/8184 Fax: 08139-8140

Tradis Verlag und Vertrieb GmbH (Bookshops)
Postfach 90 03 69, D-51113 Köln
Tel: 022 03 31059 Fax: 022 03 39340

GREAT BRITAIN

Wordsworth Editions Ltd
Cumberland House, Crib Street,
Ware, Hertfordshire SG12 9ET
Tel: 01920 465167 Fax: 01920 462267

INDIA

Om Books
1690 First Floor, Nai Sarak, Delhi 110006
Tel: 327 9823/327 4303 Fax: 327 8091

IRELAND

Easons & Son Limited
Furry Park Industrial Estate, Santry 9, Eire
Tel: 003531 8733811 Fax: 003531 8733945

ISRAEL

Sole Agent **Timmy Marketing Limited**
Israel Ben Zeev 12, Ramont Gimmel,
Jerusalem
Tel: 972-2-586 5266 Fax: 972-2-586 0035

Sole Distributor **Sefer ve Sefel Ltd**
Tel and Fax: 972-2-624 8237

NEW ZEALAND and FIJI

Allphy Book Distributors Ltd
4–6 Charles Street, Eden Terrace,
Auckland
Tel: (09) 377 3096 Fax: (09) 302 2770

MALAYSIA and BRUNEI

Vintrade SDN BHD
5 & 7 Lorong Datuk Sulaiman 7,
Taman Tun Dr Ismail,
60000 Kuala Lumpur, Malaysia
Tel: (603) 717 3333 Fax: (603) 719 2942

MALTA and GOZO

Agius & Agius Ltd
42A South Street, Valletta VLT 11
Tel: 234 038/220 347 Fax: 241 175

PHILIPPINES

I J Sagun Enterprises
P O Box 4322 CPO Manila
2 Topaz Road, Greenheights Village,
Taytay, Rizal
Tel: 631 80 61 to 66

SLOVAK REPUBLIC

Slovak Ventures sro
Stefanikova 128, 949 01 Nitra
Tel and Fax: 042 87 525105/6/7

SOUTH AFRICA

Chapter Book Agencies
Postnet Private Bag X10016
Edenvale, 1610 Gauteng, South Africa
Tel: (++27) 11 425 5990
Fax: (++27) 11 425 5997

SPAIN

Ribera Libros, SL
Poligono Martiartu, Calle 1 – no 6,
48480 Arrigorriaga, Vizcaya
Tel: 34 4 6713607 (Almacen)
    34 4 4418787 (Libreria)
Fax: 34 4 6713608 (Almacen)
    34 4 4418029 (Libreria)

UNITED STATES OF AMERICA

NTC/Contemporary Publishing Company
4225 West Touhy Avenue, Lincolnwood
(Chicago), Illinois 60646-4622, USA
Tel: (847) 679 5500 Fax: (847) 679 2494

DIRECT MAIL

Bibliophile Books
5 Thomas Road, London E14 7BN
Tel: 0171-515 9222 Fax: 0171-538 4115
Order hotline 24 hours Tel: 0171 515 9555
Cash with order + £2.50 p&p (UK)